MEETING MARY

OUR MOTHER IN FAITH

LEARNING GUIDE

CATHOLIC CENTURY

MEETING
MARY

OUR MOTHER IN FAITH

LEARNING GUIDE

Kenneth J. Howell

CATHOLIC ANSWERS
San Diego
2003

Unless otherwise noted, Scripture quotations are taken from the
Revised Standard Version: Catholic Edition (RSV:CE), copyright 1965-1966
by Division of Christian Education of the
National Council of Churches in the United States of America.

Excerpts from the English translation of the *Catechism of the
Catholic Church* for the United States of America, © 1994, United States
Catholic Conference, Inc.—Libreria Editrice Vaticana. All rights reserved.

Published by Catholic Answers, Inc.
2020 Gillespie Way
El Cajon, CA 92020
(888) 291-8000 (orders)
(619) 387-0042 (fax)
www.catholic.com (web)

Heidi Hess Saxton, ChristianWord.com, Inc., editor
Claudine and Company, cover and book design
Printed in the United States of America
ISBN: 1-888992-41-7

CONTENTS

Our Mother in Faith

It's natural to want to be close to our mothers. As small children, we depended upon our mothers for almost everything. When we grew to adulthood, we gradually distanced ourselves from the constant care and intimate companionship of our mothers to go out and make our way in life. Even so, for many people the desire to be close to Mom does not leave them.

God understands your desire for a mother. He put that desire within your very being: the need for maternal care that can be fulfilled only by having a mother who loves you, who protects you, and who is your constant companion.

Mary is such a mother for Christians. She holds a special place in the hearts of Catholics because of her unique role in God's plan of salvation. Basing its teachings on Sacred Scripture and Tradition, the Catholic Church holds that Mary was chosen to be the Mother of God. She gave the world the Redeemer. Through Mary, God gave his Son a human nature, thereby uniting heaven and earth. Mary was not simply a birth canal for the divine Son; he was given flesh from her own flesh so that, just as the rest of us are, the Son of God was "born of woman" (Gal. 4:4).

The Loving Father Gives a Loving Mother

One of the most wonderful images of God's people used in the Bible is the living reality of the family. John understood this well when he wrote, "See what love the Father has given us, that we should be called the children of God; and so we are" (1 John 3:1). Calling God "the Father" is not just a nice term to express an otherwise inexpressible idea. God truly fathers his family so that, through redemption in Christ, we become sons and daughters of the Eternal King.

If we who believe in God are a family, then our family must have a mother. What kind of family would we be if we didn't have a true mother? And who could possibly be our mother, since God did not father us in the biological sense? The biblical answer is that the Father gave us the Mother of his Son to be our Mother as well.

Paul calls Jesus Christ "the first-born among many brethren" (Rom. 8:29), and the author of Hebrews speaks of God's Son when he says, "For he who sanctifies and those who are sanctified have all one origin. That is why he is not ashamed to call them brethren, saying, 'I [the Son] will proclaim thy [God's] name to my brethren" (Heb. 2:11–12). As Jesus' brothers and sisters, we share the same parents—both Mother and Father.

Mary's motherhood of believers is suggested in the Gospel of John, where from the cross Jesus entrusts his Mother to his "beloved disciple" John. The Church recognizes that when he said to the disciple John, "Behold your mother," he was giving Mary to all of us. Like John, we are all "beloved disciples" (cf. John 19:25–27). Spiritually, we are invited to receive her as our Mother as John himself did.

And what Mary was, she continues to be. She still exercises her maternal care through the intercession she offers on behalf of us all. Loving disciples still call her "blessed among all women" (cf. Luke 1:42, 48), and invoke her as "Holy Mary, Mother of God." To understand this, we have to see the permanence of God's family.

ONCE A MOTHER, ALWAYS A MOTHER

Some events in our lives are irreversible and leave a permanent stamp on us. Perhaps you can remember such events in your life. For parents, childbirth is such a life-altering event. Some parents may try to evade their responsibilities, or even forget their children. However, they can never completely do so because bearing children leaves a permanent mark upon us. This becomes painfully evident when a parent loses a child to death. As a Protestant minister, I occasionally sat with parents in my congregation who had lost their children. I can't remember ever seeing a deeper sense of grief and loss. Our children are etched in our memories for good.

The same is true in the family of God. Once Mary gave birth to Jesus, she was and always would be his Mother. Imagine the joy Mary must have felt when the angel Gabriel told her that she would bear the Son of the Most High (cf. Luke 1:31–32). Can you sense Mary's wonder at Elizabeth's pronouncement, when Mary realized that she was bringing to her the Messiah within her own womb (cf. Luke 1:41–42)? Or the horror she must have felt when Simeon told her that she would suffer with her Son by her own soul being pierced with a sword (cf. Luke 2:34–35)? After Jesus was conceived in her womb, Mary must have known that her entire life would be marked by her intimate relationship with Jesus. Once his Mother, Mary would always be his Mother.

This reality has profound implications not only for Mary, but for us as well. The events in the lives of Jesus and Mary are more than nice Bible stories or simple historical occurrences. They represent enduring realities.

One of my favorite cable channels is the History Channel. You may have seen one of its advertising slogans, "History lives on the History Channel." Even a moment's reflection will show us how true it is that history is relevant to our everyday lives. All of us who are Americans enjoy the liberty and prosperity of the United States because of the great sacrifices of past generations. The Constitution, the great wars, and the achievements of the men and women of the past still influence us every day.

Catholicism holds that history lives in a much more profound sense than even these mundane examples show. The events of salvation history recorded in the Bible are relevant to us today. This is reflected in the *Catechism of the Catholic Church's* teaching that Mary's motherhood is a continuing reality in our lives (cf. CCC 963–972). Mary is more than the Mother of Jesus. She is our Mother in the order of grace. She is always our Mother in faith just as much as she is always Jesus' Mother. She can become our constant companion.

MARY, THE MISUNDERSTOOD MOTHER

One day I was having a conversation with an elderly man who lived next to my brother-in-law David. For some reason, the man kept calling David "Ralph." After some initial confusion, I pointed to David's house and said, "You mean the man who lives right there?" He nodded yes. "That's David's house," I said, "He's my brother-in-law. His name is David, not Ralph." The old man said, "Oh, well, we call him Ralph."

Imagine how you would feel if someone persisted in calling you by a name that is not yours. You might be forgiving at first, but you would expect him to get it right after you corrected the error a few times. To acknowledge a person's identity is to show proper respect for that person. The opposite is also true: To minimize or purposefully ignore who a person is shows disrespect.

Mary is one of the most misunderstood—and even disrespected—women in history. She has been forgotten and neglected. Her privileges have been decried, her role minimized, and her love unrequited. But Mary, as a mother, continues to love the children that God has brought into his family through baptism. As our Mother in faith, Mary wants us to love her too. But to love her, we must know her.

The most common misunderstanding of Mary outside the Catholic Church is that Catholics worship Mary. Sometimes, even when Catholics explain that they do not worship Mary, those suspicious of Catholicism still say that we make her a goddess. Others, even some Catholics, wonder if our emphasis on Mary is excessive or out of place, and if maybe those outside the Church have a point. For all these reasons, it is important to know exactly what the Church teaches about Mary and our devotion to her.

A moment's reflection makes us realize that we human beings have several different kinds of love. We certainly don't love a casual acquaintance in the same manner as a member of our family, nor our colleagues at work as we love our fellow believers. This is only natural and right. We give different kinds of respect and honor to people, depending on who they are and the nature of our relationships to them.

Long ago, the Church Fathers taught us to make distinctions between the different kinds of love that are appropriate for different kinds of people. The highest kind of love (which the Fathers called *latria*, or worship), is appropriate for God alone. Giving this kind of love to any creature is idolatry, something expressly forbidden by the first commandment (cf. Ex. 20:3–4; Deut. 5:7–8). When examining his conscience in preparation for going to the sacrament of reconciliation, every Catholic should ask himself whether he has committed the sin of idolatry. The Church Fathers insisted that *latria* could be offered only to the Triune God because he alone is worthy of worship. It is never appropriate to give this kind of love to Mary because she is a creature, and an infinite distance separates her created person from the infinite God.

For this reason, Catholics offer a special kind of love to Mary that falls short of worship. We honor her as the first and most important of the saints, a kind of love that the Fathers called *dulia*, or veneration. To grasp this kind of honor, think of Mary not in isolation from other Christians, but as the first Christian. A Christian is someone who has received Jesus Christ as Lord and Savior (cf. John 1:12). Mary can be said to be the first Christian because she was the first to say yes to the coming of Jesus.

As the first Christian, Mary is a model for every believer, an example of trust and love. She gave herself completely to God's service when she responded to the divine invitation with her words, "I am the handmaid of the Lord; let it be to me according to your word" (Luke 1:38). As her Son's disciple, she contemplated the mysteries of salvation (cf. Luke 2:19, 51). Her faithfulness shows itself by her presence at the foot of the cross (cf. John 19:25–27). So, the kind of love that is appropriate for her is the kind of love we should have for our fellow Christians. St. John makes love for fellow believers a test of our love for God (cf. 1 John 4:11).

Our love should not be limited to believers on earth today. It should extend to all God's children throughout space and time. The great Christians of past generations who have gone to heaven before us are to be honored with love and respect. Why? Because God has invited and incorporated human participation into his plan of salvation, a cooperation that evokes from us honor for his chosen servants who have lived heroic lives of holiness. The author of Hebrews details a long litany of Old Testament saints who are now in heaven (cf. Heb. 11). These saints are to be venerated by the faithful and invoked as intercessors before the throne of God.

This kind of honor is different from *latria* in that it is the honor proper to a fellow creature. It does not attribute to finite creatures the infinite goodness that belongs only to the Creator. Mary is the greatest of these saints because of her unique role in salvation history. The Church considers her to be the highest of the saints, and is accordingly honored with the highest veneration, or *hyperdulia*.

MARY, THE MANY-SIDED GEM

We show Mary the kind of honor and love that we do because of who she is. Though Mary is first and foremost our Mother, she is also much more. As the Church has reflected on Mary for centuries, the tongues of the faithful have sung her praises with many titles. The traditional prayer entitled "The Litany of Blessed Virgin Mary" is one among many such poetic expressions. It emphasizes Mary as Mother, Virgin, and Queen.

The early Christians loved the oxymoron involved in calling Mary Virgin and Mother. How can a woman be both a virgin and a mother? The impossible becomes a window into the many sides of Mary. She alone among women is both a pure Virgin and a true Mother. As a virgin, Mary acts as a sign of how miraculous God's salvation is. As a mother, Mary's receptive heart shows us how to be open to God's love.

MARY AND JESUS

In this book, we want to learn about Mary from watching her Son Jesus Christ. Our primary source for learning about Jesus is, of course, the Bible, and especially the four Gospels: Matthew, Mark, Luke, and John. In the following lessons, we will reflect on all that Sacred Scripture teaches about Jesus and Mary.

Scripture is not the only source of our knowledge about Mary. The Catholic Church also bases its beliefs on the unbroken traditions concerning Mary that have been handed down from generation to generation. We know of these traditions from the writings of the Church Fathers and other teachers of the faith who have transmitted them to us for two thousand years. The liturgies and the prayers of the Church also show us the Church's belief in Mary's unique relationship with Jesus. All these sources indicate one essential point: Mary should be at the very heart of a Catholic's daily life.

If we can learn about Mary by looking at Jesus, it is also true that we can learn about Jesus by looking at Mary. Mary is like a mirror because her life reflects her Son's life. The more we learn of her, the more we find her reflecting the heart of Jesus. An amazing transformation takes place when we peer more deeply into Mary's life. We also become like her, a mirror reflecting the glory of the Lord. St. Paul understood this well when he wrote, "And we all, with unveiled face, beholding the glory of the Lord, are being changed into his likeness from one degree of glory to another; for this comes from the Lord who is the Spirit" (2 Cor. 3:18).

Come now and let us explore the heart of this tender Mother, this beautiful woman who, more than any other, has completely embodied God's love. As we look into her loving eyes, we will see a heart like no other, a soul that—alone among women—has been declared by heaven to be "full of grace" (Luke 1:28).

THE LITANY OF THE BLESSED VIRGIN MARY

The Litany of the Blessed Virgin Mary, a major expression of veneration, contains fifty ways to address Mary and ask for her intercession:

Holy Mary, Holy Mother of God, Holy Virgin of virgins, Mother of Christ, Mother of divine grace, Mother most pure, Mother most chaste, Mother inviolate, Mother undefiled, Mother most amiable, Mother most admirable, Mother of good counsel, Mother of our Creator, Mother of our Savior, Virgin most prudent, Virgin most venerable, Virgin most renowned, Virgin most powerful, Virgin most merciful, Virgin most faithful, mirror of justice, seat of wisdom, cause of our joy, spiritual vessel, vessel of honor, singular vessel of devotion, mystical rose, tower of David, tower of ivory, house of gold, Ark of the Covenant, gate of heaven, morning star, health of the sick, refuge of sinners, comforter of the afflicted, help of Christians, Queen of angels, Queen of patriarchs, Queen of prophets, Queen of apostles, Queen of martyrs, Queen of confessors, Queen of virgins, Queen of all saints, Queen conceived without original sin, Queen assumed into heaven, Queen of the most holy rosary, Queen of peace.

STUDY QUESTIONS

Answers to multiple-choice, true/false, and factual-answer questions are found at the end of the book in Appendix 5.

1. The Church believes Mary was chosen to be the Mother of God based on what evidence?

   a) She is the only human being who ever gave the world a Redeemer

   b) Mary gave to the Son of God his human nature, thereby uniting heaven and earth

   c) The teachings in Sacred Scripture and Tradition

   d) All of the above

2. What is the most common misunderstanding of non-Catholics regarding Catholics' relationship with Mary? What can we do to counter this misunderstanding?

   _____

   _____

   _____

   _____

   _____

3. What are the distinctions taught to us by the Church Fathers regarding the different kinds of devotion: *latria*, *dulia*, and *hyperdulia*? _____

   _____

   _____

4. The first Christian to receive Jesus as her Lord and Savior

   was _____ .

5. Studying Mary in Scripture, how can we imitate Mary and

   thus draw closer to Christ? _____

   _____

   _____

   _____

   _____

6. A good way to honor Mary is by:

   a) Saying the rosary daily

   b) Reading *True Devotion to Mary*, by Louis

      de Montfort

   c) Imitating her

   d) All of the above

MARY IN GOD'S PLAN OF SALVATION

WOMEN HAVE PLAYED enormously important roles in world history, but those roles have not always been recognized. We may hear of Cleopatra and Jane Addams, Queen Victoria and Eleanor Roosevelt, but rarely do we hear of the countless women who have nurtured famous children at their breasts and taught them at their knees.

If there ever was a woman who did not seek the limelight, it was Mary. Her humility allowed her to be content with an anonymous place in God's plan. Yet, no woman ever played so crucial a role in history. In this lesson, we will explore the indispensable role Mary played in God's saving plan.

In the first lesson, we emphasized that Mary is a spiritual mother given to us by God the Father so that we may experience the love of his Son, Jesus Christ. The key to understanding Mary, then, is to understand her relationship to Jesus. The Fathers of the Second Vatican Council understood this well when they emphasized that everything we believe about Mary comes from what we believe about Christ. This central fact will aid us in keeping a balance between underestimating Mary's significance and overemphasizing her position in the order of grace.

Mary Receives Jesus
in Her Heart and Body

The place to begin is Sacred Scripture, particularly the New Testament, since it is in its pages that we may see most clearly Mary's relationship to Jesus Christ. Mary's story begins even before Jesus was born. Luke tells us in his Gospel that the angel Gabriel was sent by God to visit Mary, a virgin already engaged to a man named Joseph (cf. Luke 1:26–27).

Mary was disturbed—a natural human reaction—by this angelic visit (cf. Luke 1:30). When Gabriel told her she would give birth to the Son of God, her fear turned to bewilderment. She knew that she had never had sexual relations with Joseph, much less any other man. How could she, a virgin, give birth to "the Son of the Most High" (Luke 1:32)?

Gabriel told her that the Holy Spirit would "come upon you, and . . . overshadow you" (Luke 1:35). Now Mary could understand the unique and wonderful gift that God wanted to give her: an opportunity to be God's vessel in carrying out his will. No other woman in history had ever been given that opportunity.

If we carefully attend to Luke's language in telling this event, we will see several important features of Mary's life. Mary appears as a normal Jewish woman with all the natural human thoughts and feelings. We are told "she was greatly troubled at [Gabriel's] saying, and considered in her mind what sort of greeting this might be" (Luke 1:29). On this basis the Church affirms that Mary was no goddess, no superhuman woman. Mary would have known that Gabriel's words "the Lord is with you" (Luke 1:28) had also been addressed to God's servants of old when God was asking them to undertake some great mission.

The words "Hail, full of grace" were also astonishing. How could an angel from God use words of such dignity to an unknown and insignificant woman? We will return to this greeting in Lesson 6, but for now we can simply note the high dignity bestowed on Mary by God. Elizabeth, her elderly relative, had recognized that dignity when she exclaimed, "Blessed are you among women, and blessed is the fruit of your womb!" (Luke 1:42).

By Gabriel's words, Mary was being set apart and exalted as

Mary was born to
Sts. Joachim and
Anne, probably
between 15 and
20 B.C. Early tradi-
tions assert that
the birth of Mary
came about
through the fer-
vent prayers of
Joachim and Anne
in their advanced
age. They gave her
the name Miryam,
which was a
popular name
among first-cen-
tury Jews. In most
ways, Miryam may
not have appeared
to be different
from many other
young Jewish
women. The An-
nunciation of the
angel Gabriel
changed all that.
At the time of the
Annunciation,
Mary was living in
Nazareth, a city in
Galilee.

the greatest woman in the history of God's plan. And why?
Why Mary, the unknown daughter of Joachim and Anne?
Mary's humble response provides the answer: "Behold, I am
the handmaid of the Lord; let it be to me according to your
word" (Luke 1:38). This is an ancient way of saying, "God, I
am totally yours and am at your disposal completely." Now we
see why God dignified Mary with the title "Full of Grace." Her
humility was not some self-deprecating sentimentality. It consisted in being totally available to God.

If an angel had bestowed on you words of such dignity the
way Gabriel did to Mary, would you not have begun to feel
that you were someone special? The reaction would have been
completely understandable. But the fullness of grace that was
in Mary shows itself again in the mission she immediately un-
dertook. She did not glory in her exalted position. Instead, she
humbly submitted to God's will. Luke tells us that she also
went to her relative Elizabeth to share in Elizabeth's joy in carrying John the Baptist.

The story of the Visitation (cf. Luke 1:39–56) emphasizes
the joy of the encounter between these two holy women. As
Luke tells the story, Mary had no sooner arrived than Elizabeth
recognized the presence of the Lord within Mary's womb. It
would have been customary for Mary to give deference to her
much older relative, since pious Jewish people honored the elderly. Yet, we find that it is Elizabeth who defers to Mary by saying:

Blessed are you among women, and blessed is the fruit of
your womb! And why is this granted me, that the mother of
my Lord should come to me? (Luke 1:42–43).

Elizabeth acknowledged the divine presence within Mary
and experienced the movement of her own son within herself
as a sign of joy. Out of this encounter we find Mary offering
God a hymn of joy—the Magnificat, a song of praise that has
shaped Catholic devotion from the earliest days of the Church.

Mary's hymn reveals much about her. It shows us how she
was filled with God's presence and grace. She begins, "My soul
magnifies the Lord, and my spirit rejoices in God my Savior"
(Luke 1:46–47).

To magnify means to make something bigger. But how can
anyone make God bigger than he already is? The key to understanding *magnify* is to see its parallel. "My soul magnifies"

parallels "my spirit rejoices." The second phrase refers to an interior joy within Mary's heart, and the first does something similar. Mary's soul is filled up with God. Gabriel called her "full of grace," but now we find what that grace consisted of. Her heart is full of the Lord himself. It is this fullness of the Lord's presence in Mary that makes her both different from us and like us. Her ability to magnify the Lord arose from the superabundance of grace in her. We can and do have God's grace, but she had it in the fullest measure possible.

Why did she magnify the Lord? Luke 1:48 tells us: "For he has regarded the low estate of his handmaiden." With these words Mary identifies with the humble position of her people Israel. Throughout the Old Testament, a godly woman who identifies with the people of God is always praised. Queen Esther and Judith are two prime examples. The entire hymn speaks of Mary's concern for her people. When Mary proclaims in verses 50–55 that God has overturned the pride of the rich and rewarded the poor, she sums up this wonderful truth by saying that God "has helped his servant Israel, in remembrance of his mercy, as he spoke to our fathers, to Abraham and to his posterity for ever" (Luke 1:54–55).

The Jewish people of Mary's time were under the yoke of Roman domination. She identified with her people, thus fulfilling the type of the Old Testament women who completely and totally gave themselves to the welfare of God's people. This posture of taking up the cause of God's people was the first step in Mary's becoming our spiritual Mother. The Church is now the New Covenant people of God with whom Mary identifies.

Mary saw herself as a "Daughter of Zion," a term used by the prophets to designate God's people. She is a personal embodiment of Israel: a poor and humble daughter, but a daughter whom God has favored. With her conception of Jesus in her womb, the Daughter of Zion now holds the Son of Zion, the perfect Israelite. God's chosen daughter now carries God's own Son.

MARY WALKS WITH JESUS

Many Christians seem to think that Mary's role in the life story of Jesus can be forgotten after his conception and birth. However, her role extended beyond giving birth. She lived her entire life in devotion to her Son. This fact is seen clearly in two passages in the Gospel of John.

Mary appears at the beginning of Jesus' ministry. At the wedding feast in Cana, Mary plays the role of intercessor (cf. John 2:1–11). She teaches us the utmost importance of obeying Jesus her Son. Just as she told the servants, so she is telling us, "Do whatever he tells you" (John 2:5).

Mary also intercedes for the couple when she makes her implicit request that Jesus provide wine for them (cf. John 2:3). This intercessory role is an extension of her maternal role. As Mother, she mediated God's presence to us on earth. As intercessor, she mediates our requests to God in the person of Jesus, the Son of God.

The other story in which Mary plays an important role in John's Gospel is the account of the Crucifixion. In John 19:25–27 we read that Mary and "the disciple whom [Jesus] loved" were standing beside Jesus' cross along with some other women. All of those present at Jesus' dying moments came of their own free will. All chose to come. Their presence suggests that their faith was strong, that they willingly chose to share in Jesus' sorrows.

Yet it was Mary alone who had been told that she would experience this kind of suffering because of her unique relationship to Jesus. When she and Joseph presented the infant Jesus in the Temple, the old man Simeon told only her that "this child is set for the fall and rising of many in Israel, and for a sign that is spoken against (and a sword will pierce through your own soul also), that thoughts out of many hearts may be revealed" (Luke 2:34–35). Because of Simeon's prophecy, Mary's presence at Jesus' Crucifixion takes on a deeper significance. Mary was not only chosen to conceive and give birth to God's Son, but she was destined to suffer with him, too.

Jesus and Mary are inseparable. Once united by the power of the Holy Spirit, their lives were intertwined forever. Mary conceived Jesus in her womb, but only after she had agreed in her heart to God's plan ("Let it be to me," Luke 1:38). Mary brought Jesus to the world. Mary was there at the beginning of his public ministry in Cana (cf. John 2:1–11). Mary stood by him in his dying moment at the cross (cf. John 19:25–27).

A Tale of Two Women: Eve and Mary

In those two passages in John's Gospel, at the wedding feast and at the cross, we find a word used of Mary that has great importance for understanding her place in God's plan. In both stories she is called simply "woman."

When his Mother asks Jesus to intervene at the wedding in Cana, Jesus replies, "O woman, what have you to do with me? My hour has not yet come" (John 2:4). Again in John 19:26, as Jesus is dying on the cross, he entrusts Mary to John with the simple words, "Woman, behold your son!" Why does Jesus not use his Mother's name? Or just call her "Mother"?

Jesus' use of the word *woman* signals Mary's unique role in taking the place of Eve, the first woman. The book of Genesis tells us how Eve cooperated with Adam, the first man, plung-

---

The Fathers Know Best: On the New Eve

"By disobeying, [Eve] became the cause of death for herself and the whole human race, so also Mary ... was obedient and became the cause of salvation for herself and the whole human race.... Just as the human race was subject to death by a virgin, it was freed by a virgin, with the virginal disobedience balanced by virginal obedience."

St. Irenaeus, Bishop of Lyons
Against Heresies (second century)

"Here there is a great mystery that life was born through a woman since death had also come to us through a woman. This was so that the devil might be conquered by crucifixion in both sexes, female and male."

St. Augustine
On Christian Combat (fourth century)

"Death by Eve, life by Mary."

St. Jerome (fourth century)

---

ing mankind into the mire of sin. The apostle Paul tells us in Romans 5:12–21 and 1 Corinthians 15:21–22, 45 that Christ became the second Adam because he undid the plight of sin and death that Adam brought on us.

The Church Fathers, following Paul's example, drew out a further implication. They knew that just as there was a second Adam, so there was a second Eve. A man and woman brought sin into the world, and a man and woman brought us out of sin.

Augustine also said that the New Testament was hidden in

the Old and that the Old Testament was revealed in the New. Mary's role was hidden in the pages of the Old Testament. By comparing the Old with the New, we come to appreciate Mary even more. Mary's role, assigned to her by God, was to be that unique woman who undid the tangled mess that Eve created by her sin.

MARY AND THE ONGOING WORK OF SALVATION

Can you now see why the Catholic Church honors Mary so highly? It is because the Church takes the Scriptures seriously and listens to the wisdom of the Church Fathers with a humble ear. Mary is unique among women because her Son is unique among mankind.

Mary's role in God's plan is not limited to the past, just as Jesus did not come to be a historical relic of the past. His mission was not to be remembered as a good teacher. His saving work continues today as men and women learn to trust him, as they learn to love him, and as they come to the Church he founded. Since Mary is inseparably tied to Jesus, her role as Mother continues and her ministry to God's children endures.

Mary stands before us as an example of how we should receive the grace of God. In following her example, we become Christ's coworkers in the salvation of our fellow human beings. Like Mary, we are recipients of grace. The work of bringing salvation to others is primarily God's work; we cannot do it ourselves. So we must receive grace in order to give grace. Once we are recipients of grace, we are transformed into conduits of grace, channels through which Christ's loving mercy can flow. By understanding Mary, we come to see our own place in God's plan of salvation.

EVE AND THE NEW EVE IN THE BIBLE

"'I will put enmity between you and the woman, and between your seed and her seed; he shall bruise your head, and you shall bruise his heel.' To the woman he said, 'I will greatly multiply your pain in childbearing; in pain you shall bring forth children'" (Gen. 3:15).

"And a great portent appeared in heaven, a woman clothed with the sun, with the moon under her feet, and on her head a crown of twelve stars; she was with child and she cried out in her pangs of birth, in anguish for delivery" (Rev. 12:1).

STUDY QUESTIONS

Answers to multiple-choice, true/false, and factual-answer questions are found at the end of the book in Appendix 5.

1. What we believe about Mary comes from what we believe about Christ.

   TRUE _____   FALSE _____

2. In her hymn of joy, the Magnificat, with whom does Mary identify? _____

3. Read Genesis 3:15. What did the Church Fathers discover in this passage about Mary's role in salvation history?

   _____

   _____

   _____

   _____

4. Mary's role in God's plan of salvation ceased after Jesus' birth.

   TRUE _____   FALSE _____

5. Who interceded between the couple and Jesus at the wedding in Cana? What miracle was the outcome of her intercession? _____

   _____

6. How does the miracle in Cana encourage us to ask for

Mary's intercession? _____

_____

_____

_____

_____

THE MOTHER OF GOD

IS IT ALL too good to be true? Do you hesitate to believe in Mary as your Mother, unable to believe that God would offer you such a wonderful gift? Some people are skeptical simply because they cannot imagine God the Father having love so great that he would give them a Mother in faith. Others find it difficult to imagine this kind of maternal love because they never experienced real love from their own mothers. That is a sad reality. However, for these very reasons the heavenly Father gave us all a Mother's love. The woman whom God meant to be our Mother in the order of grace is also the Mother of God.

We emphasized earlier that Mary played a unique role in the history of salvation since she alone gave birth to the Redeemer of the world. However, in other ways many biblical figures played unique roles as well. In the proper sense, only Moses can be credited as Israel's Lawgiver; only Jeremiah is the weeping prophet; only John the Baptist is herald of the Messiah.

Mary's uniqueness lies in her relation to the Savior Jesus Christ. All the Old Testament figures pointed forward to Christ in varied ways. All the New Testament apostles and martyrs witnessed to Christ with their words and lives. Yet, it was only Mary who gave the Messiah flesh of her flesh, and in doing so she became the Mother of God. In this lesson we want to explore the meaning of Mary's divine maternity.

MARY'S DIVINE MOTHERHOOD IN SCRIPTURE

Let us begin with the foundation of Scripture and delve more deeply into its meaning. In the last lesson we saw how Luke drew attention to the divine presence in Mary's womb. Elizabeth, Mary's elderly relative, exclaimed, "Blessed are you among women, and blessed is the fruit of your womb! And why is this granted me, that the mother of my Lord should come to me?" (Luke 1:42–43).

These words "the mother of my Lord" must have shocked many first-century Jews, who would have understood that the phrase was being applied to a divine being—in other words, to God. This was clearly Luke's intent, if we look more closely at the language of the Annunciation narrative.

MARY: ARK OF THE NEW COVENANT

In addition to being the New Eve, Mary fulfills other types in the Hebrew Bible as well. One of these types is not a person, but a sacred object: the Ark of the Covenant.

The ark was a box made from acacia wood that was overlaid with gold and carried on poles by the priests of Israel. It contained the "testimony"—the two tablets containing the Ten Commandments, which God had given Moses on Mount Horeb (cf. Ex. 40:20; Deut. 10:2). On top of the ark were two golden cherubim who spread their wings over the mercy seat (cf. Ex. 25:10–22). They symbolized the heavenly cherubim who praise the mercy of God day and night (cf. Is. 6:1–3). Later, Aaron's rod that budded was added (cf. Num. 17:1–11).

It was an unmistakable symbol of God's word and presence. In 2 Samuel 6:2 we read of "the ark of God, which is called by the name of the Lord of hosts who sits enthroned on the cherubim."

The Ark of the Covenant was lost during the Babylonian exile and has never been found to this day. Judaism later applied the term *ark* to the box in synagogues that hold the Torah scroll. Thus, they continued the association between the word of God and the ark.

Like the Ark of the Covenant, Mary carried the Word of God within her. Through her Son, she manifested the presence of God just as the ark symbolized God's presence.

In his narration of the Annunciation, Luke relates how Gabriel told Mary that her Son would be called "Son of the Most High" (Luke 1:32), a title indicating his divine origin.

This climaxes in the declaration:

> The Holy Spirit will come upon you, and the power of the Most High will overshadow you; therefore, the child to be born will be called holy, the Son of God (Luke 1:35).

Here Luke uses carefully selected language to show the divinity of the child to be born. The word *overshadow* is just one example. The Greek word *episkiasei* comes from a root meaning "a shadow or a cloud" and is used of the visible cloud that descended over the tabernacle and the Temple in the Old Testament. Both tabernacle and Temple were the places of God's special and intimate presence (cf. Ex. 40:34–38;1 Kgs. 8:10, 13), a kind of dwelling of God on earth.

In our Lukan text, the Holy Spirit is promised to descend over Mary, a temple of the Most High God. Yet, in the Old Testament, God not only descended over the Temple; he also resided in the Temple. So also, in the New Testament, the Holy Spirit descends on Mary to bring the presence of one "called the Son of God."

There can be no doubt about Luke's meaning. He intended for us to understand Jesus as God in Mary's womb. Matthew complements Luke's perspective by speaking of Jesus as "Emmanuel" or "God with us." In the story of Jesus' birth, Matthew quotes and emphasizes the classic passage from Isaiah 7:14: "Behold, a virgin shall conceive and bear a son, and his name shall be called Emmanuel" (Matt. 1:23).

Matthew translates the Hebrew name of the child, Emmanuel. It means "God is with us." Now from the point of view of the ancient prophet Isaiah, the birth of this child may have been a sign of God's presence in general. However, as Matthew interprets the prophecy, he makes it clear that it is the child himself who is God with us, not just a name applied to an otherwise human child.

Matthew's focus on Joseph underscores this fact. Joseph's perplexity at Mary's pregnancy is relieved only when he learns that the child comes from the Holy Spirit (cf. Matt. 1:20). When Joseph was commanded to call the child Jesus, he must have realized the profound role the child was to play in God's plan, for Jesus is a Greek transliteration of the Hebrew name Yeshua or Yehoshua, meaning "Yahweh is salvation." These biblical texts all point to the same conclusion. The child in Mary's womb is God, a fact that Elizabeth understood under the inspiration of the Spirit (cf. Luke 1:41). Her calling Mary "the mother of my Lord" then would be audacious, even blasphemous, if it were not true. But then, if it is true, it is even more astounding. How can an ordinary woman be the Mother of God? How can a poor Jewish girl give birth to God? The history of the Church shows that there would be others who had difficulties with the idea of a woman bearing God.

THE BATTLE AT EPHESUS: A CRUCIAL TURNING POINT

As anyone who has ever read military history knows, there are crucial turning points in war, moments that decide the outcome of an entire campaign. Sometimes the significance of these moments can be fully appreciated only in retrospect. The history of the Church shows the same pattern. At times, the entire future of Christianity has hung in the balance; only through painful battles has the Church survived and thrived.

The year A.D. 431 was such a turning point. In that year, a great number of bishops gathered in the ancient city of Ephesus to determine whether Mary could be properly called the "Mother of God." Nestorius, the bishop of Constantinople, had stirred the controversy by preaching against calling Mary *Theotokos*, or "God-bearer." Nestorius insisted that Mary was not the Mother of Jesus' divine nature but only his human nature, and that she should therefore be called the *Christotokos*, or "Christ-bearer." The fierce reaction to Nestorius shows that the early Christians had become very comfortable with calling Mary the Mother of God, or *Theotokos*. Why should they now give up this precious term of affection for Mary?

The main opponent of Nestorius was the great orator St. Cyril of Alexandria. Cyril addressed the Council of Ephesus in 431, persuading them that Mary ought to retain her title as the Mother of God. In his speech, Cyril proclaimed:

> Mary, Mother of God, we salute you. Precious vessel, worthy of the whole world's reverence, you are an ever-shining light, crown of virginity, the symbol of orthodoxy, an indestructible temple, the place that held him whom no place can contain, Mother and Virgin. Because of you the holy Gospels could say: Blessed is he who comes in the name of the Lord.

We do not know if Cyril and Nestorius ever debated in person, but the imaginary dialogue that follows certainly expresses the differences between their views:

Nestorius: We cannot say that Mary is the Mother of God, the *Theotokos*, because she did not give birth to God. How can God be given birth by a woman? No, Mary is the *Christotokos*, the Christ-bearer. She gave birth to the human Jesus.

Cyril: You are right. Mary gave birth to the Christ, the Messiah. However, Scripture teaches that Christ was God in Mary's womb. "The Word became flesh and dwelt among us." The Church has always believed this.

Nestorius: Jesus Christ is God, but it was not his Godhead that Mary bore. It was only his humanity.

Cyril: Your position, Nestorius, is not what the Church has taught. We have always honored Mary as the Mother of God. Listen to the words from our liturgy by our holy father John Chrysostom: "It is truly right to bless you, *Theotokos*, the ever blessed and completely pure Mother of our God. You are more honorable than the Cherubim, and incomparably more glorious than the Seraphim. You gave birth to God the Word without corruption. We magnify you as the true *Theotokos*." Do not these words make it clear what the Church has always believed?
Furthermore, if you believe that Jesus was fully God, but that Mary bore only the humanity of Christ in her womb, then you must answer this question: When did Jesus the man become God if he was not God in Mary's womb?

Nestorius: I say that Jesus was God in Mary's womb, but that Mary had nothing to do with his divinity. She cannot therefore be called the Mother of God.

Cyril: But think of what you are saying, Nestorius. If you say that Mary gave birth only to the man Jesus, then you are also saying that there were two people in Mary's womb— one God and one man. But our faith, based on Holy Scripture, is that Jesus Christ is the true God-Man, not two separate persons, but two natures in one person. Further, a mother does not give birth to a nature, but to a person. Jesus Christ is unique because he has two natures, but he is still only one person.

Christians have always honored Mary as the Mother of God. They painted pictures on the walls of the catacombs in the days of persecution before the emperor Constantine permitted Christianity. In the catacombs of Priscilla in Rome, one can see these early depictions of Mary holding the divine child in her arms. Mary contributed only to Jesus' human nature, but what emerged from her womb was not just a human Jesus, but God in the flesh. She is the Mother of his human nature, but she can rightly be called the Mother of God because she carried a person who was God in her womb.

Mary, Mother of God and Our Mother

The Christians of Cyril's day were persuaded by his arguments not because he was such a clever man, or a powerful orator. It was because they could see from Scripture that Jesus must have been God in Mary's womb. They also realized that throughout history Christians had held that Mary was the *Theotokos*, the God-bearer, and that it was necessary to preserve this tradition, which had been handed down from the apostles. They also believed it because they could clearly see that if Mary were not the Mother of God, then they were left with a Savior who was really not God in the flesh.

About twenty years after the Council of Ephesus, Pope Leo the Great sent a letter to the next ecumenical council meeting at Chalcedon to affirm the decision of the Council of Ephesus. Thereafter, devotion to Mary under the title *Theotokos*, or Mother of God, spread far and wide throughout the Church.

Nestorius was not the last Christian to struggle with this truth. However, it has remained the constant teaching of the Church since apostolic times. Consider this: If Mary did not have the second Person of the Trinity united to our humanity in her womb, then there really was no such person as the God-Man. And if there is no God-Man, then there can be no union between God and man. Because God chose to redeem the human race through the sacrifice of his incarnate Son, the only way for us to be united with him is for him to unite himself to our humanity. Every Mass reminds us of this truth in the prayer of the priest as he mixes the wine and water in the chalice: "By the mystery of this water and wine, may we come to share in the divinity of Christ, who humbled himself to share in our humanity."

We have only one Savior who is "the way, and the truth, and the life" (John 14:6). He can be the way to the Father only if he is fully God and fully man. The woman who brought us this perfect God-Man is the same one who loves us today as a Mother.

STUDY QUESTIONS

Answers to multiple-choice, true/false, and factual-answer questions are found at the end of the book in Appendix 5.

1. What is the significance of Elizabeth's greeting to Mary in Luke 1:42–43?

2. Mary is often referred to as the Ark of the New Covenant. Compare the Ark of the Old Covenant with Mary, the Ark of the New Covenant.

3. What does the Greek word *episkiasei* mean, and what did the evangelist want us to understand by using that term in Luke 1:35?

4. The Council of Ephesus was important because:

   a) It ultimately decided the nature of Mary

   b) It ultimately decided the nature of Jesus

5. What do the terms *Christotokos* and *Theotokos* mean, and why is applying the correct term to Mary important?

   _____

   _____

   _____

   _____

   _____

6. How does the mingling of the water and the wine relate to the mystery of the Incarnation?

   _____

   _____

   _____

   _____

THE MOTHER OF THE CHURCH

EVERY SUNDAY, MILLIONS of Catholics all over the world receive Holy Communion. Every week at Mass the sacrifice of Christ on the cross is made present in our churches. But what does this act of communion mean? Why do we receive the body and blood of Christ in the Eucharist? And what does this communion have to do with Mary?

Communion began with Mary in that she made our communion with Christ possible. Holy Communion is the union of a human being with God through the sacred humanity of Christ. That union of Christ and our humanity began in the womb of the Virgin Mary.

By becoming the Mother of God, Mary became our Mother at the same time. As we said earlier, once Mary became Jesus' Mother, she is always his Mother. The *Catechism of the Catholic Church* reminds us of this when it says, "Mary's role in the Church is inseparable from her union with Christ and flows directly from it" (CCC 964). Every time we receive Jesus Christ in the sacred host at Communion, we are also sacramentally receiving Christ with the human nature that he took from Mary.

The New Motherhood of Mary

"And so this 'new motherhood of Mary,' generated by faith, is the fruit of the 'new' love, which came to definitive maturity in her at the foot of the cross, through her sharing in the redemptive love of her Son" (RM 23).

MARY AND THE CHURCH: AN UNBREAKABLE BOND

If Mary and her Son are inseparable, then Mary is also inseparable from the life of the Church, because Christ cannot be separated from his Church (cf. Rom. 8:35–39). This connection between Mary and the Church was evident to the earliest Christians, who embraced Mary in the earliest days of the Church.

The burial catacombs of St. Agnes in Rome contain a large fresco from the early centuries of Christianity depicting Mary with her arms outstretched, holding St. Peter in one hand and St. Paul in the other. The picture of these two great pillars of the Church in Mary's arms shows how the leaders of the Church have long seen themselves as children of Mary. That same tradition continues to the present day.

In his encyclical *Redemptoris Mater* ("Mother of the Redeemer"), John Paul II taught that "Mary belongs indissolubly to the mystery of Christ, and she belongs also to the mystery of the Church from the beginning, from the day of the Church's birth" (RM 27). How then is Mary linked to the Church? John Paul sees her silent but powerful presence as most important. Mary was not one of the twelve apostles, but her presence in prayer with the apostles on the day of Pentecost meant that she was in the heart of the Church. "She was present among them as an exceptional witness to the mystery of Christ" (RM 27).

John Paul's teaching is based on Acts 1:14: "All these with one accord devoted themselves to prayer, together with the women and Mary the mother of Jesus, and with his brethren." The Pope teaches that as "the Church became fully aware of the mighty works of God on the day of Pentecost" (RM 26), Mary's presence in the heart of the Church witnessed to the work of the Holy Spirit that had already begun in her at the Annunciation. In a sense, the Church was beginning the journey in the Spirit that Mary had begun over thirty-three years before. Mary then led the way for the apostles, even though her maternal influence was quiet and gentle.

In 1988, John Paul II issued *Mulieris Dignitatem* ("On the Dignity and Vocation of Women"), a letter in which he spoke again about Mary's maternal role. The Pope reflected deeply on the message contained in story of the Annunciation. Mary calls herself "the handmaid of the Lord" (Luke 1:38), an expression that echoes later in Jesus' words, "For the Son of man also came not to be served but to serve" (Mark 10:45). The Pope pointed out the connection between these two expressions as evidence that "Mary takes her place within Christ's messianic service" (MD 5). In this way, Mary gives a human example to the Church that "to serve . . . means to reign" (LG 36). The Church is called to be the servant of God, to understand that the way to glory comes from serving (cf. Mark 9:35).

MARY ACTS AS OUR MOTHER

If Mary is the Mother of the Church, what role does she play in raising her children? Mary's motherhood shows itself in the example she provides for us as her children. A mother needs to instruct her children, just as Mary instructed the servants on the day when Jesus turned water into wine. As John relates the story (cf. John 2:1–11), we hear Mary telling Jesus, "They have no wine." Jesus then asks Mary, "O woman, what have you to do with me?"

As Jesus prepares to perform the miracle, Mary turns to the servants and says, "Do whatever he tells you." Part of the reason that John told us this event is for us to remember that we are to be Jesus' servants, ready to do his bidding. Mary then functions as a Mother who teaches us to follow Jesus.

Mary's greatest example is in the way she lived her life. From her very first appearance in Scripture, Mary is a person who is docile to the will of God. Her famous fiat, "Let it be to me according to your word" (Luke 1:38), becomes an example of total surrender to God that is intended to inspire all of us. Her example as Mother extends throughout her life as well. She joined in the sufferings of her Son. The old prophet Simeon foretold of her sufferings when Joseph and Mary presented Jesus in the Temple. We read Simeon's prophecy:

> Behold, this child is set for the fall and rising of many in Israel, and for a sign that is spoken against (and a sword will pierce through your own soul also), that thoughts out of many hearts may be revealed (Luke 2:34–35).

Mary chose to unite herself with her Son in his sufferings when she stood at the cross with the beloved disciple (cf. John

19:25–27).

The story of Mary at the foot of the cross beautifully illustrates Mary's motherhood of all.

As the *Catechism of the Catholic Church* so beautifully says (cf. CCC 964), Mary's motherhood extends to all people because Jesus' death on the cross was for all people. If you read John 19:25–27 carefully, you will see how Jesus tells the beloved disciple to receive his Mother. First, Jesus speaks to

MOTHER OF MYSTERY

Undoubtedly, we find here an expression of the Son's particular solicitude for his Mother, whom he is leaving in such great sorrow. And yet the "testament of Christ's cross" says more. Jesus highlights a new relationship between Mother and Son, the whole truth and reality of which he solemnly confirms. One can say that if Mary's motherhood of the human race had already been outlined, now it is clearly stated and established. It emerges from the definitive accomplishment of the Redeemer's Paschal Mystery.

The Mother of Christ, who stands at the very center of this mystery—a mystery that embraces each individual and all humanity—is given as Mother to every single individual and all mankind. The man at the foot of the cross is John, "the disciple whom he loved." But she is not given to John alone. Following tradition, the Council does not hesitate to call Mary "the Mother of Christ and Mother of mankind": since she "belongs to the offspring of Adam, she is one with all human beings. . . . Indeed she is 'clearly the mother of the members of Christ . . . since she cooperated out of love so that there might be born in the Church the faithful'" (RM 23, cf. LG 53–54; St. Augustine, *De Sancta Virginitate*, VI, 6: PL 40, 399).

Mary, saying, "Behold, your son." In this, Jesus is telling Mary to consider John—who, as the beloved disciple, represents all of Christ's disciples—as her own son. Then Jesus speaks to John, saying, "Behold, your mother." In this second part, Jesus is telling John to think of Mary not only as a fellow disciple, but as his own Mother. This is confirmed in the next verse when he says, "From that very hour, the disciple received her as his own." This verse is sometimes translated as "From that hour he took her to his own home."

While this second translation is possible, the first translation fits better with the context of John's Gospel. Two facts in verse 27 confirm this translation. First, the verb *lambanein* can mean either "take" or "receive." It is the same verb used in John 1:11–12, where it clearly means "receive." These verses read:

MEETING MARY

"He came to his own [*eis ta idia*] home, and his own people received [*parelabon*] him not. But to all who received [*elabon*] him, who believed in his name, he gave power to become children of God."

It is consistent with the meaning of John 1:11–12 to translate *lambanein* in John 19:27 as "receive." Moreover, the phrase translated "as his own" or "into his own home" is the same Greek phrase (*eis ta idia*) used in John 1:11, where John clearly means "to his own." It is consistent with John 1:11 to translate this phrase in John 19:27 "to his own" rather than "into his own home."

Translation of an author's meaning frequently requires comparing the same words used by the author in different contexts. The better translation of John 19:27 is: "From that very hour, he [the disciple] received her as his own [mother]."

God inspired John to record this story as an example to us that we may do what John did— namely, receive Jesus' Mother as our own Mother. We know this from the use of John's self-description of "the beloved disciple." John intends this title not only for himself, but for all Jesus' disciples. Mary is given to us by Jesus to be our Mother in faith.

> ## All True Devotion Leads to Christ
>
> "The history of piety shows how 'the various forms of devotion toward the Mother of God that the Church has approved within the limits of wholesome and orthodox doctrine' have developed in harmonious subordination to the worship of Christ, and have gravitated toward this worship as to their natural and necessary point of reference. The same is happening in our own time. The Church's reflection today on the mystery of Christ and on her own nature has led her to find at the root of the former and as a culmination of the latter the same figure of a woman: the Virgin Mary, the Mother of Christ and the Mother of the Church. And the increased knowledge of Mary's mission has become joyful veneration of her and adoring respect for the wise plan of God, who has placed within his family (the Church), as in every home, the figure of a Woman, who in a hidden manner and in a spirit of service watches over that family" (MC 3, cf. LG 6).

DEVOTION TO MARY AS THE MOTHER OF THE CHURCH

All that we have said about Mary's motherhood of the Church beckons us to love her. In every healthy family, the children have a special affection for their mother. As a natural father, I know how happy it makes me when I see my children showing affection and honor for their mother, my wife. When we have love for Mary, we are in step with generations of Christians who have learned that growth in faith leads to growth in love for the Mother of God.

In 1974, Paul VI introduced *Marialis Cultus* ("On Devotion to Mary"), his apostolic exhortation on devotion to Mary. In this document, the Pope underscored how love for Christ and love for Mary are intertwined (see inset).

As we increase in love for Christ, we increase in love for Mary. Our communion in the holy gifts of the Eucharist becomes far more meaningful when we understand that the body that Mary conceived in her womb is the same body we receive in the Holy Eucharist.

Mary, as the Mother of the Church, continues to feed us with the same Christ she once bore. And without a divine-human Savior, there would be no Communion for us to receive. The next time you walk the aisle of the church to receive Communion, thank Mary, who made your communion possible. In later lessons, we will explore even more how Mary's motherly care is greater than we can imagine.

Study Questions

Answers to multiple-choice, true/false, and factual-answer questions are found at the end of the book in Appendix 5.

1. The early Church recognized the connection between Mary and the Church.

   TRUE _____   FALSE _____

2. The words that Jesus used to establish a mother-son relationship between Mary and the beloved disciple are:

   _____

   _____

3. How did the beloved disciple receive Mary?

a) As Jesus' Mother

b) As his own Mother

4. Who is the disciple Jesus loves?

_____

5. Every time we receive Jesus Christ in the sacred host at

Communion we receive _____

_____ .

6. According to the *Catechism* (964), if Mary and Jesus are

inseparable, then Mary is also inseparable from the life of

the Church. What New Testament verse makes this

connection between Mary and the Church?

_____

_____

_____

_____

_____

MARY, EVER VIRGIN

EVERY SUNDAY, AT the beginning of Mass, Catholics pray a prayer of confession that goes like this:

> I confess to Almighty God
> and to you, my brothers and sisters,
> that I have sinned through my own fault,
> in my thoughts and in my words,
> in what I have done and what I have failed to do.
> And I ask the Blessed Mary, Ever Virgin,
> all the angels and saints, and you, my brother and sisters,
> to pray for me to the Lord our God.

Why do we pray this prayer of confession instead of moving straight into worship? And why do we invoke the saints instead of addressing God directly as we worship? Finally, why speak of Mary as "Ever Virgin" when asking her to pray for us? The prayer also asks "all the angels and saints, and you, my brothers and sisters" to join us in this prayer, but it does not qualify these latter people by any such phrase. Of all the things that could be said of Mary, why is it her perpetual virginity that is mentioned?

In this lesson, we will explore the practical importance of believing in Mary's perpetual virginity as well as why the Church so firmly proclaims this truth.

MARY'S VIRGINITY
BEFORE JESUS' BIRTH

Since the earliest days of Christianity, the Church has taught that Mary was a virgin not only before she conceived her Son, but after his birth and for the rest of her life as well. In order to explain why the Church has always taught this, we must once again begin with Scripture. What does it tell us about the Mother of Jesus?

Understanding Mary's lifelong virginity requires understanding her virginity before Jesus was born. When we look at Scripture, our first impression is that the virginity of Jesus' Mother is clear. Matthew tells the story of Jesus' birth in the following words:

> Now the birth of Jesus Christ took place in this way. When his mother Mary had been betrothed to Joseph, before they came together she was found to be with child of the Holy Spirit. . . . All this took place to fulfill what the Lord had spoken by the prophet: "Behold, a virgin shall conceive and bear a son, and his name shall be called Emmanuel (which means, God with us)" (Matt. 1:18, 22–23).

The other Gospel writer who treats Jesus' birth, Luke the physician, also clearly indicates that Mary is a virgin in the exchange between her and the angel Gabriel (cf. Luke 1:34). When Gabriel tells Mary that she will give birth to a son who will be David's descendent and who will rule over God's people, Mary does not understand how such a thing is possible. The words she uses are literally, "I do not know man" (Luke 1:34).

Gabriel tells her that this conception and birth will be miraculous: "The Holy Spirit will come upon you, and the power of the Most High will overshadow you; therefore the child to be born will be called holy, the Son of God" (Luke 1:35). This exchange makes clear what Gabriel intended, and what Mary understood: that her Son would not be conceived by means of human sexual intercourse. And the miraculous circumstances of his birth fit perfectly with the miraculous nature of the one born to Mary—fully God, yet fully man. The very nature of the Messiah as the Son of God makes fitting his entrance into this world by a supernatural means.

Almost no Christians doubted that Jesus was born of a virgin before modern times. Even today, Mary's virginity before the birth of Jesus is universally accepted by nearly all Christians. It is only since about the eighteenth century that modern skepticism began to question this doctrine. However, the official teaching of the Catholic Church has never wavered. The rejection of this doctrine is based on a naturalistic bias that reads the Bible as if it were like any other human document.

Sometimes, one hears skeptics assert that the Bible does not teach the Virgin Birth. For example, the Hebrew word used in Isaiah 7:14 for virgin is *almah*, a word that usually means "young woman," and not necessarily a virgin. Thus, it is argued, Isaiah did not intend this woman to be understood as a virgin. However, since Scripture does not contradict itself, we must assume that Matthew's use of *parthenos* to translate *almah* affirms the virginity of Mary, since *parthenos* can mean only "virgin." Thus, by comparing one scriptural text with another, we see that the Bible fully intends for us to understand Mary's state before and in Jesus' birth as being virginal.

MARY'S VIRGINITY AFTER JESUS' BIRTH

Catholics believe not only that Mary was a virgin when she conceived Jesus Christ in her womb, but that she remained a virgin throughout her life. For some Christians this belief in Mary's perpetual virginity presents a difficulty. They do not see statements in Scripture to indicate this to them, and they do not usually think that there is a good reason for it. Why wouldn't Joseph and Mary have had marital relations? Since there is nothing immoral about a husband and a wife having sexual relations, why would Mary and Joseph refrain?

The Catholic Church maintains that the perpetual virginity of Mary is a tenet of faith that cannot be given up. The Church also affirms that sexuality is blessed by God and that it is good. Yet the Church holds that in the case of Mary and Joseph, a special situation made it fitting that they refrain from normal marital relations.

WHAT ABOUT THE "BRETHREN OF THE LORD"?

Certain biblical texts are sometimes used to deny Mary's life-long virginity. These texts are taken out of the context of Scripture and Christian history. It is important to bear in mind that ancient Church Fathers also knew of these biblical texts, and yet they still believed that Mary was always a virgin. So we must ask ourselves: How did the first Christians interpret these passages, and why? Let us examine two texts that are commonly cited as evidence against Mary's perpetual virginity.

1. *Jesus calls his disciples his brothers and sisters in Mark 3:31–35 (with a parallel in Matthew 12:46–50):*

> And his mother and his brethren came; and standing outside they sent to him and called him. And a crowd was sitting about him; and they said to him, "Your mother and brethren are outside, asking for you." And he replied, "Who are my mother and my brethren?" And looking around on those who sat about him, he said, "Here are my mother and my brethren! Whoever does the will of God is my brother, and sister, and mother."

On the surface, this passage seems to suggest that Jesus had a family the same way everyone else does, and that Mary had other children. But a closer look suggests problems with this interpretation. If Jesus could speak of those who do God's will as his "brother, and sister, and mother," then he clearly was not using the words in the most literal sense. His disciples are not his blood brothers and sisters, and yet he calls them by these titles. Even if Jesus were using the terms literally (instead of metaphorically, as he appears to be doing here), the terms for "brothers" and "sisters" had a range of meaning much broader than they do in English.

The Church Fathers commonly offered two explanations for who the "brethren of the Lord" were. One was that these siblings—like those mentioned by name in Matthew 13:55–56 (James, Joseph, Simon, and Judas)—were children of Joseph by a previous marriage and therefore were Jesus' stepbrothers. Some in the ancient Church held that Joseph was considerably older than Mary, and that he had probably died before Jesus began his public ministry. This explanation accords with the curious absence of Joseph in the Gospels after Jesus was twelve years old (cf. Luke 2:41–52). This tradition is recorded as early as the year A.D. 120, in a document known as the *Protoevangelium of James*, which emphasizes the perpetual virginity of Mary.

The stepbrothers account was the standard explanation of who the brethren of the Lord were until the time of Jerome, in the fifth century, who popularized the second explanation: The "brethren" were not immediate family at all, but were more distant relations, such as cousins. This is based on the expanded range of meanings of the Greek term *adelphos* and the corresponding Hebrew term *ach*. Sometimes these terms were used to refer to other close relatives: cousins, nephews, and nieces, among others.

For example, in Genesis 12:5, Lot is called Abram's brother's son (i.e., nephew), but in Genesis 13:8, Abram says to Lot, "Let there be no strife between you and me . . . for we are kinsmen." The word for "kinsman" is the Hebrew word for "brother," *ach*. Likewise, the Gospel writers, although they wrote in Greek, were mostly Jews who used Jewish manners of speech. Thus, in the Bible, *brother* and *sister* are not always used to mean actual blood relations. This means that Jesus' brothers and sisters mentioned in the Bible may be more distant relatives, such as cousins.

All the Church teaches is that they were not Mary's biological children. They may have been her stepchildren, adopted children, or even more distant relations, such as nieces and nephews. In addition to the reasons listed above, there is the passage from John 19:26 to consider. If there had been a closer blood relative to care for Mary, why would the Lord have entrusted his Mother to the beloved disciple?

2. *Joseph "knew her not until she had borne a son" (Matt. 1:25).*

This is another text that is often cited to argue against Mary's perpetual virginity. Matthew is clearly using the word *know* in the biblical sense of "having sexual relations." The English translation makes it sound as if Joseph did not have relations with Mary until Jesus was born but that he did have relations with her after Jesus' birth.

This is not a new objection. A man named Helvidius first raised it in the fifth century, provoking a response from the greatest Scripture scholar of the ancient Church, Jerome. He pointed out that the Greek word used for "until" (*heos*) simply does not require that an action happened *after* a certain point, but only that it did not happen before that point.

Jerome's explanation was so impressive that both of the greatest leaders of the Protestant Reformation saw no problem in affirming Mary's perpetual virginity (see inset on Martin Luther). One of these, John Calvin, the reformer of Geneva, called anyone who denied Mary's perpetual virginity a "contentious trouble maker." He pointed out in his commentary on Matthew 1:25 that it speaks only about what happened up until Jesus was born, not after he was born.

Calvin's and Luther's attitudes are important. Even though they broke away from the Church, they retained a healthy respect for many ancient Christian teachings. Although this respect for tradition is not so evident in many non-Catholic churches today, these Protestant leaders recognized the value of listening to the wisdom of Christians who had come before them. They accepted Mary's perpetual virginity and did not see it as contradicting Scripture. They believed, as we should, that these teachings, long accepted by the people of God, were in fact guided by the Holy Spirit as Jesus promised (cf. John 14:26; 15:26; 16:13). Scripture and Tradition from ancient times consistently affirm Mary's perpetual virginity.

Luther on Mary's Virginity

Even Martin Luther, the father of Protestantism, believed in Mary's virginity: "It is an article of faith that Mary is Mother of the Lord and still a virgin.... Christ, we believe, came forth from a womb left perfectly intact" (Weimer's *The Works of Luther*, English translation by Pelikan, v. 11, pp. 319–320; v. 6. p. 510).

WHY IS MARY
THE EVER VIRGIN?

Mary's perpetual virginity does not contradict the Bible, as some Christians think, just as no Catholic doctrine contradicts the Bible. Yet the mere fact of Mary's perpetual virginity tells us very little about the importance of this truth or about its practical import. To answer the question of why Mary's constant virginity is important, we must return to the basic idea expressed in previous lessons: namely, that there exists an inseparable link between Jesus and Mary, an intimate relation-

THE FATHERS KNOW BEST:
ON THE PERPETUAL VIRGINITY OF MARY

Here are just a few of the many testimonies to the universal belief among early Christians that Mary not only gave birth to Jesus as a virgin, but remained a virgin her entire life.

"Remembering our most holy, pure, blessed, and glorious Lady, the *Theotokos* and ever virgin Mary, with all the saints, let us commit ourselves and one another and our whole life to Christ our God."

> St. John Chrysostom (fourth century), in a prayer from the Orthodox and Eastern rite liturgy

"It helps us that the evangelist says about the first-born and the only begotten that she stayed a virgin 'until she gave birth to her son, her firstborn.' For Mary, who is more honored and noble than all, was neither married to anyone nor did she ever become a mother to any other. After the birth, she remained a pure virgin always and perpetually."

> Didymus the Blind (fourth century), in his treatise on the Trinity

"A virgin in conception, a virgin in giving birth, a pregnant virgin, fruitful virgin, a perpetual virgin."

> St. Augustine (fifth century), Sermon 186, 1

"She conceived as a virgin, she gave birth as a virgin, she remained a virgin."

> Pope Leo the Great (fifth century)

ship that grows out of Mary's call to be the Mother of God.

It is hard to imagine a more difficult calling than Mary's. She was called not only to give birth to the Messiah, but to watch her divine Son suffer the insults, rejection, and hatred of the world. This was a task that no ordinary woman could bear in her own power. Mary needed grace. She received grace at her conception in her mother's womb and she cooperated with that grace throughout her life. What gave her the strength she needed to cooperate with God's grace? It was very simply her purity of heart.

Every time she said yes to God (cf. Luke 1:38), she confirmed the grace of God already given to her. Every time she did some little act of self-denial, she grew in the strength she needed to face the ultimate trial—her Son's death on the cross (cf. John 19:25–27). It was this purity that gave her the strength. This purity of heart is reflected in her commitment to lifelong virginity. So Mary's remaining a virgin all her life fit her special calling to be the Mother of God.

Another reason for Mary's perpetual virginity has to do with us, her children. In previous lessons, we stressed how Mary's maternal love for all Christians helps us to know and love Jesus Christ better, and to grow in perfection as Jesus has called us (cf. Matt. 5:48). This involves acknowledging our sin, repenting of it, receiving Christ's forgiveness and endeavoring to live in accord with God's law. That is why the Church asks us to confess our sins at the outset of every Mass.

In order to grow in grace as fully as possible, we should always ask the help of God's servants (angels and saints) to intercede for us, that we might learn to live holy lives. That is why focusing on Mary as the "Ever Virgin" is important. Her perpetual virginity witnesses to her purity of heart, without which she never could have lived a perfect life. Her constant, perpetual assent to the will of God gave us an example of what purity of heart looks like. We know this to a lesser degree from experience when we see other holy people around us. Their example of purity spurs us on to be holy. How much more is this true of the one woman whose purity of heart constantly and repeatedly assures us that we too can say yes to God's will by the help of his grace.

There is still more. Earlier we stressed Mary's motherhood of believers. And yet, there is also symmetry between Mary's virginity and her motherhood. As Mary is always a virgin, so she is always a mother. Her perpetual virginity is matched by her perpetual maternity. We ask Mary the Ever Virgin Mother to pray for us because her prayers are effective weapons in our struggles against sin. They draw us deeply into the sacred heart of Jesus.

"Blessed Art Thou ..."

"This union of the mother with the son in the work of salvation is made manifest from the time of Christ's virginal conception up to his death; first when Mary, arising in haste to go to visit Elizabeth, is greeted by her as blessed because of her belief in the promise of salvation and the precursor leaped with joy in the womb of his mother; then also at the birth of our Lord, who did not diminish his mother's virginal integrity but sanctified it" (LG 57).

STUDY QUESTIONS

Answers to multiple-choice, true/false, and factual-answer questions are found at the end of the book in Appendix 5.

1. The doctrine of Mary's perpetual virginity was never seriously doubted before the eighteenth century.

   TRUE _____ FALSE _____

2. What are Catholics to believe about Mary's virginity?

   a) Mary was a virgin when she conceived Jesus in her womb

   b) Mary remained a virgin throughout her life

   c) Both a and b

3. What evidence do we have that the Greek-speaking churches believed in Mary's perpetual virginity?

   _____

   _____

4. Two Protestant reformers who believed in Mary's perpetual virginity were _____

   _____ .

5. Mary's perpetual virginity is a witness to her purity of heart. In which of the following ways does this help us?

   a) It makes Mary a role model for us

b) It gives us confidence to ask for her intercession

c) It gives us hope in our attempts to become holy

d) All of the above

6. Our faith is replete with paradoxes, one being Mary's perpetual virginity coupled with her universal motherhood. Can you think of some other paradoxes of faith? _____

_____

_____

_____

_____

THE IMMACULATE CONCEPTION

So FAR WE have seen Mary as a mother and virgin. Like the early Church Fathers, we should marvel at the juxtaposition and rejoice in the paradox. How could the same woman be a virgin and a mother? The very impossibility of this in the natural order was evidence for the divine origin of Christ, for only God could bring about the Virgin Birth. In this lesson, we explore another great miracle of God's grace, and in that miracle we discover Mary's incomparable blessings.

To prepare this young Jewish woman to bear the Redeemer, God the Holy Spirit applied the merits of Jesus' death to Mary's heart from the moment she was conceived in her mother's womb. This unique act, known as the Immaculate Conception, made her a fitting vessel of God's grace, and protected her from the ravages of sin. This plenitude of grace was signaled by the angel Gabriel when he addressed her as "full of grace" (Luke 1:28).

The dogma of the Immaculate Conception is often misunderstood, resulting in people neglecting or rejecting its truth. In this lesson we will explore the meaning of the dogma by first looking at how the Pope defined it when it was proclaimed an infallible teaching. Then we will see the basis for the doctrine in the Bible and the history of Christian thought. This knowledge will aid us to see the practical importance of this doctrine.

The Meaning of the Papal Definition

On December 8, 1854, Pope Pius IX declared and defined the Immaculate Conception as a dogma of the faith all Catholics are obliged to believe (see inset). The Immaculate Conception refers to Mary, who was conceived in her mother's womb without original sin or its stain. There are several unique features about this dogma that we must grasp if we are to see its importance and implications.

In order to understand the significance of this dogma, take a look at the third chapter of Genesis, the story of the Fall of Adam and Eve. The rest of the Bible shows ample evidence that Adam and Eve's decision to disobey God affected the entire human race (cf. Rom. 5:12–21). Every human being comes into this world with original sin because Adam and Eve lost their state of blessing not only for themselves but for their descendants as well.

Theologically speaking, original sin is the deprivation of sanctifying grace, which God restores in us at baptism. Every human being also has an inclination to sin called concupiscence. This inclination to sin is part of what is called the "stain" (Latin, *macula*) of original sin. Both original sin and its stain are transmitted from parent to child.

The dogma of the Immaculate Conception means that, at the very moment when Mary was conceived in her mother's womb—at that moment when original sin and its stain would have been transmitted to her—God protected Mary so that she would be free from original sin and its stain (making her *immaculate*, or "unstained").

How was this possible, since every human being is a sinner? The papal document explains that God gave Mary a special grace and privilege because of the enormous responsibility that she would carry as the Mother of the Redeemer. Mary played a unique role in giving birth to and raising Jesus. We saw in earlier lessons how this singular task required of Mary more than any normal human being could naturally do. Nevertheless, God asked Mary to do this, and God never asks his servants to do anything without supplying the grace with which to do it. And so Mary received the grace proportionate to her calling to be the Mother of God. The grace she received was to

Immaculate Mary

"By the authority of Jesus Christ our Lord, of the blessed apostles Peter and Paul, and by our own: We declare, pronounce, and define that the doctrine that holds that the most Blessed Virgin Mary, in the first instance of her conception, by a singular grace and privilege granted by Almighty God, in view of the merits of Jesus Christ, the Savior of the human race, was preserved free from all stain of original sin, is a doctrine revealed by God and therefore to be believed firmly and constantly by all the faithful" (*Ineffabilis Deus*).

be free from the ravages of original sin that affect every other human being.

The only way for Mary to be exempt from original sin was through what her Son Jesus Christ accomplished later on the cross. This is what Pius IX meant by the phrase "in view of the merits of Jesus Christ, the Savior of the human race." Mary's Immaculate Conception resulted from the perfection of Christ's sacrifice. Mary was saved through Jesus' atoning sacrifice, just as we are. In our case, this sacrifice of the cross is applied to individuals throughout the course of our lives, through the sacraments and through prayer. In Mary's case, the same sacrifice was applied at one moment of time: at her conception.

How did the Church come to this conviction? Mary's Immaculate Conception is based on Scripture and Tradition.

A KEY TITLE: FULL OF GRACE

In Lesson 2, we read and discussed the story of the Annunciation, when the angel Gabriel announced to Mary that she had been chosen to be the Mother of God. Let us now return to that historic event as recorded in Luke 1:26–38. The language of the Annunciation is full of rich meaning. Luke 1:28 tells us that, when Gabriel approached Mary, he said, "Hail, full of grace, the Lord is with you." These apparently ordinary words are anything but commonplace.

The first word from the angel is *hail*, a term used in ancient times when an inferior spoke to a superior. So, in ancient Rome it was common to say, "Hail, Caesar." We hear people mocking Jesus in phrases used of great leaders, "Hail, King of the Jews" (Matt. 27:29). This is a strange word used by an angel to a young Jewish woman of fifteen or sixteen years of age. Here an angel from the presence of God speaks to Mary as if she were his superior. Why would Gabriel use such a term of deference?

When Gabriel approached Mary, he said, "Hail, full of grace, the Lord is with you." This was an extraordinary greeting. We might have expected Gabriel to say, "Hail, Mary" as Catholics say in the rosary, or as our examples above said. But Gabriel does not use Mary's name; he says "Hail, full of grace." The phrase "full of grace" describing Mary is one Greek word, *kecharitomene*. Older English translations follow the ancient

Vulgate Latin phrase *gratia plena*.

A number of modern translations, both Catholic and Protestant, have changed "full of grace" to "highly favored one" or some similar phrase. Although many modern scholars argue that "highly favored" is a better translation, there are many good reasons to retain the older translation "full of grace." The form of the word in Luke 1:28 derives from a Greek verb, *charitoo*, which is used only one other time in the New Testament, in Ephesians 1:6. The root word means "to make one favored" or "to give one grace."

In its grammatical form, *kecharitomene* has something special to convey. It must not be confused with a phrase found in some English versions of Acts 6:8, where Stephen is said to be "full of grace and power." The phrase in that verse is different in Greek (*pleres charitos kai dunameos* instead of *kecharitomene*). The grammatical form of the word applied to Mary—*kecharitomene*—is a perfect passive participle. We don't have perfect passive participles in English, so let me explain. You may have to think back to your high school grammar classes for a second, but it won't be too hard.

Participles are adjectives that are based on verbs. In this case, *kecharitomene* is based on the verb *charitoo*, or "to grace." You can do anything with a participle that you can do with an adjective, including using it as a description of someone. That is what is happening here: Gabriel is describing Mary and her graced condition.

The fact that the verb is *passive* also tells us something: Mary's graced condition isn't something she is producing; it is something done for or given to her by someone else (i.e., by God). The fact that the tense is *perfect* is also informative. In Greek, the perfect tense describes actions in the past that have been completed but have continuing effects in the present. This tells us about how Mary has been graced: The grace the angel is speaking of is something that was given to her in the past—it has already happened—but it has continuing effects in the present, when Gabriel is speaking to her.

There is one final bit of grammar to *kecharitomene* that is significant for our purposes: It is a form of the word that is used when directly addressing someone. (This is known as the "vocative case" because you use it to *invoke* someone.) Gabriel thus isn't just describing Mary, saying "God has really graced you"; he's using *kecharitomene* as a direct address, almost as a title.

Translations like "highly favored one" don't capture all of this. If one wanted to give a contemporary English translation that seeks to reflect the term's different aspects, one might use "One Who Has Been Graced." However, the traditional translation "full of grace" does this admirably.

It is important to underscore that "full of grace" is passive. Many non-Catholic authors mistakenly think that the phrase "full of grace" means that the Catholic Church teaches that Mary is an independent source of grace to others. Nothing could be further from the truth. Mary's being "full of grace" means that she was filled with grace by God the Father, grace that flowed from the redemptive merits of her Son. Mary was a vehicle of grace because she was an instrument of bringing Christ into the world.

So, the angel used "full of grace" (*kecharitomene*) to call attention to Mary's state before God because of the unique role that she was about to play in giving birth to the Messiah. Rather than refer to her natural name, Mary, the angel meant her to understand that the thing that characterizes her above any other is her uniquely graced state.

THE CHURCH'S INSIGHT GROWS

In earlier lessons, we saw the importance of looking to the wisdom of the historic Church to see what God's people have always believed. We did this because we believe that Christ did not abandon the Church but promised to lead her into all truth through the Holy Spirit teaching the apostles. This Holy Spirit, called "the Spirit of truth" by Jesus (cf. John 14:17; 15:26; 16:12), is promised as the one who will remind the apostles of Jesus' words (cf. John 14:26; 15:26). Jesus explicitly promised that this Spirit will "guide you into all the truth" (John 16:13).

So, let us find out what truths the Holy Spirit has confirmed to the historic Church about Mary's Immaculate Conception. One clear witness to this teaching comes from St. Ephrem the Syrian (d. 373), who composed several hymns to Mary in the fourth century. In one of these Ephrem wrote:

You alone and your Mother
are more beautiful than any others;
for there is no blemish in you,
nor any stains upon your Mother.
Who of my children
can compare in beauty to these?

Ephrem witnesses to the faith of the Syriac-speaking Christians with regard to Mary's blameless life. Similarly, the liturgy or worship of the Church shows how the early Christians thought. Long before the Immaculate Conception was defined, the liturgy of the Church spontaneously sang of Mary's purity. In the Byzantine Catholic liturgy of John Chrysostom (fourth century), we hear the Church singing:

Let us commend ourselves, one another
and our whole life to Christ our God,
As we remember the all-holy, immaculate,
highly blessed, and glorious Lady
who is our *Theotokos*, the Ever Virgin Mary.

In the previous lesson, we noted that this prayer testifies to the early Church's faith in Mary's perpetual virginity ("Ever Virgin Mary"). But it also shows faith in Mary's immaculate heart. In the same breath that speaks of Christ as God, it radiates a respect for Mary as the one who is "all holy" or "completely holy" (*panagia*). And, lest we have any doubts about the extent of this holiness, the Greek liturgy uses the word *achrantos*, which means "immaculate."

These two witnesses to Mary's purity could be multiplied many times over. However, these examples should demonstrate that, when Pius IX defined the Immaculate Conception as a dogma of the faith, he did not do so in a vacuum. The Church of the present always looks back to see how the Holy Spirit has led the Church in the past to attain true understanding.

WHY IS THE IMMACULATE CONCEPTION IMPORTANT?

We have seen the roots of the Immaculate Conception in Scripture and a little of how this doctrine developed over time in the history of the Church. At one level, this should be enough to convince us of the necessity of this teaching, but it is also valuable to explore how Mary's being immaculately conceived fits into the plan of salvation. Let us go back to the fundamental biblical idea that God is all-holy and human beings are sinners.

If, as is clear in Scripture, God wanted to dwell and live among his people, then the question arises of how this holy God could do so without compromising his holiness. The Old Testament prepared the way by showing that God purifies the place where he comes to dwell. The Ark of the Covenant was consecrated and set aside as a special place for God to dwell with his people (cf. Ex. 25:22). On the ark were fastened cherubim that modeled the cherubim of heaven because the ark was to be an earthly representation of heaven (i.e., a place where God would dwell).

The holiness of God shows up again in 2 Samuel 6: the story of David bringing the ark to Jerusalem. There we find the combination of awe and joy among God's people, who realize the holiness of God and marvel that God would bring his presence among them. The ark is an instrument of bringing the presence of God.

Mary is the Ark of the New Covenant. She brings into the world the presence of God, the all-holy Redeemer. Yet, how could God's chosen Ark of the New Covenant bear the all-holy Jesus in her womb while tainted with sin—both original sin and sins of her own doing? In the Old Testament, we find just the opposite: "Wisdom will not enter a deceitful soul, nor dwell in a body enslaved to sin" (Wis. 1:4).

The story of the Visitation (Luke 1:39–56) has strong parallels with the story of the ark coming to Jerusalem. There is no doubt that Luke wished us to see Mary as the Ark of the New Covenant. This is one reason why Mary's sinlessness was main-

---

KEPT BY THE GRACE OF GOD

"According to the belief formulated in solemn documents of the Church, this 'glory of grace' is manifested in the Mother of God through the fact that she has been 'redeemed in a more sublime manner.' By virtue of the richness of the grace of the beloved Son, by reason of the redemptive merits of him who willed to become her Son, Mary was preserved from the inheritance of original sin.

In this way, from the first moment of her conception—which is to say of her existence—she belonged to Christ, sharing in the salvific and sanctifying grace and in that love that has its beginning in the 'Beloved,' the Son of the Eternal Father, who through the Incarnation became her own Son" (RM 10).

tained in the wake of the Gospels. Some early Christian documents—for example, the *Odes of Solomon* (A.D. 80) and the *Protoevangelium of James* (A.D. 120)—state that Mary bore Christ without the pain of childbirth. This shows how early Christians believed that Mary was free of the curse that had been placed upon the first Eve (cf. Gen. 3:16).

We began this lesson by noting that the Immaculate Conception is poorly understood, even by Catholics. The more we understand Mary's privilege, the more we see the glory of Christ her Son. His perfect life, sufferings, death, and resurrection are the source of Mary's purity of heart. We depend on these things for our own purity of heart as well—since we know that only the pure in heart will see God (cf. Matt. 5:8).

STUDY QUESTIONS

Answers to multiple-choice, true/false, and factual-answer questions are found at the end of the book in Appendix 5.

1. The Immaculate Conception refers to:

   a) Jesus being conceived in Mary's womb through the power of the Holy Spirit

   b) Mary's freedom from original sin before her birth

   c) Mary's being conceived in her mother's womb without original sin

2. On December 8, 1854, the Catholic Church began teaching that Mary was immaculately conceived.

   TRUE _____   FALSE _____

3. Concupiscence means:

   a) The tendency to sin

b) Being born without original sin

c) Being born with original sin

4. What does the Greek word *kecharitomene* mean?

_____

_____

5. How is it possible that Mary was saved from original sin when Christ was not yet born?

_____

_____

_____

_____

6. How does Mary's Immaculate Conception relate to us?

_____

_____

_____

_____

THE ASSUMPTION AND QUEENSHIP

THERE WAS ONCE an innocent man who was imprisoned for many years. During his long sojourn behind bars, he never gave up his determination to be free again. When a fellow prisoner once asked him if he ever wavered in his resolution to be free, he responded that hope is a good thing, maybe the best of things. The Christian faith agrees. Hope is a good thing. In fact, hope is one of the best three things mentioned in Scripture: "So faith, hope, love abide, these three" (1 Cor. 13:13).

Human beings can live without a lot of things, but they cannot live without hope. Our Lord understands this deep human need. Mary's Assumption into heaven is one of our greatest sources of hope. The Assumption of Mary shows us the power of Christ's Resurrection and Ascension. It gives us a glimpse of our own destiny in Christ, for as Paul writes, at the Second Coming "the dead in Christ will rise first; then we who are alive, who are left, shall be caught up together with them in the clouds to meet the Lord in the air; and so we shall always be with the Lord. Therefore comfort one another with these words" (1 Thess. 4:16–18).

THE ASSUMPTION OF MARY
DEFINED BY PIUS XII

It is crucial that we understand the meaning of Mary's Assumption if we are to see its practical import. The Assumption was the last of the four major Marian dogmas to be infallibly defined by the Church. The significance of this fourth dogma is best understood in the light of the other three: the divine maternity (*Theotokos*), perpetual virginity, and especially the Immaculate Conception.

In the last lesson, we studied how Mary's Immaculate Conception flowed from the death of her Son on the cross. Without his death, Mary could not have been conceived without the stain of original sin. The Assumption is similar to the Immaculate Conception in that Mary experienced in advance an aspect of salvation that is promised to all believers. Mary was the first to experience being raised to the side of Christ, something that has been promised to all faithful followers of Jesus.

Mary's Assumption is related to Jesus' Resurrection and Ascension as her Immaculate Conception is related to his death. As the Immaculate Conception shows the perfection of Jesus' dying on the cross, the Assumption shows the perfection of his rising from the dead. Christ died on Calvary to make us completely pure (i.e., immaculate), but this goal is accomplished over the course of a believer's life. In Mary's case, Jesus' death made her immaculate instantaneously, when she was conceived in her mother's womb.

Similarly, it is because of Jesus' Resurrection that we too shall be raised at the end of time. In Mary's case, the power of Jesus' Resurrection raised Mary to heaven, body and soul, at the end of her earthly life. Mary's Immaculate Conception explains how she was saved from sin by Jesus in a unique way. Mary's Assumption shows the immediate union of her whole being with God at the end of her life.

Mary's Assumption was infallibly proclaimed in 1950. On August 15 of that year, Pope Pius XII issued *Munificentissimus Deus*, a document that defined the Assumption of Mary as a dogma of faith that all Catholics are obliged to believe. The title of this encyclical hints at its importance. It means "the most generous God"; Mary's Assumption was a demonstration of the overflowing generosity of God. This fact points us to a basic truth about God and his saving love for humanity.

On what basis did Pius XII decide to define this dogma? The proclamation was not an invention of erudite theologians or overly pious minds, but a fundamental expression of Christ's saving grace. The Pope affirmed something God had already done: God, out of the love he has for human sinners, gave them an unmistakable sign of his generous intentions toward them. The great Triune God wishes us to live with him forever in our full humanity, body and soul. By taking Mary up to heaven body and soul, God the Father showed us that he intends us to live with him in the bliss of our glorified humanity. Pius XII explained it in this way:

> The Mother of God, mysteriously united from all eternity with Jesus Christ in the one and the same decree of predestination, immaculate in her conception, a virgin inviolate in her divine motherhood, the wholehearted companion of the divine Redeemer who won complete victory over sin and its consequences, gained at last the supreme crown of her privileges—to be preserved immune from the corruption of the tomb, and like her Son, when death has been conquered, to be carried up body and soul to the exalted glory of heaven, there to sit in splendor at the right hand of her Son, the immortal king of the ages (*Munificentissimus Deus* 40).

This document connects the Assumption preeminently with Christ and the other aspects of Mary's life. Among other things, Pius XII notes the biblical pattern of suffering that leads to eternal glory. As the old prophet Simeon had predicted, "A sword will pierce through your own soul also" (Luke 2:35). Mary's heart was pierced as she witnessed Jesus' suffering on the cross (cf. John 19:25–27).

As Paul teaches in Romans 8:17 and 2 Timothy 4:6–8, suffering in this life is rewarded by God in the next. The Assumption reminds us that, as Mary suffered with her Son, so she also shares in his glory. So belief in the Assumption is a source of hope for Christians, because it foreshadows what will one day happen to each faithful Christian. We will all be like Mary is now, taken body and soul into heaven.

How Was Mary Taken into Heaven?

The key wording in Pope Pius XII's declaration: "Having completed the course of her earthly life, [Mary] was assumed body and soul to heavenly glory." In the century before he declared it, popes had received petitions from 113 cardinals; 250 bishops; 32,000 priests and religious brothers; 50,000 religious women; and eight million lay people, all requesting that the Assumption be infallibly defined as a Catholic teaching.

The Pope discerned that the Holy Spirit was speaking through the people of God on this matter.

THE ASSUMPTION OF MARY IN THE HISTORY OF THE CHURCH

Pius XII did not invent this doctrine. He proclaimed it as an expression of the faith of the whole Church. His declaration was a response to the people of God, who asked him to infallibly define the Assumption (see inset). Even then, it was not enough to have the consent of the faithful. The doctrine had to be grounded in the history of Christian belief. It had been accepted by bishops, reinforced by papal teachings, and believed by Christians for centuries.

One way we discover how Christians thought about the Assumption is by looking at the history of liturgy. In seeing how Christians have worshiped, we see their beliefs. This is known as the principle of *lex orandi, lex credendi*: "The prayer of the Church is the rule of faith."

Belief in the Assumption goes back to the earliest centuries and over the course of time came to be expressed in the Church's liturgy. We know that the Assumption has been celebrated in the liturgy at least since the seventh century. The *Gregorian Sacramentary* is believed to have originated from Pope St. Gregory I (d. 604). In this liturgical book we find the collect (opening prayer) for the Mass mentioning Mary's Assumption indirectly. In another book entitled *Missale Gallicanum Vetus*, we find that the Church in seventh-century Gaul (modern France) had an Assumption Mass. Later in that century, Pope Sergius (687–707) ordered a solemn procession for the feast of the Assumption.

Nor was the Assumption limited to the Western Church. In the East, the Greek-speaking Church called the feast the Dormition (Falling Asleep) of Mary. The Byzantine Emperor Maurice ordered a solemn procession for the feast on August 15. By the eighth century we have sermons on the feast, including those of the great St. John of Damascus:

> It was necessary that she who had preserved her virginity inviolate in childbirth should also have her body kept free from all corruption after death. It was necessary that she who carried the Creator as a child on her breast should

dwell in the tabernacles of God. It was necessary that the bride espoused by the Father should make her home in the bridal chambers of heaven. It was necessary that she, who had gazed on her crucified Son and had been pierced in the heart by the sword of sorrow which she had escaped in giving him birth, should contemplate him seated with the Father. It was necessary that the Mother of God should share the possessions of her Son, and be venerated by every creature as the Mother and handmaid of God.

What these witnesses indicate is how God's people, both clergy and laity, grew to understand more deeply Mary's Assumption over a long period of time. The quotation above from St. John of Damascus shows one such profound reflection. As ancient Christians grew in their understanding of Mary's unparalleled blessings as the Mother of God, they grasped that Mary's being assumed was a natural consequence of her being immaculately conceived and supernaturally protected by God.

In fact, if she was completely pure throughout her life, free from original and actual sin, then it would have been an unnatural consequence for her to die in the usual way, because death is the result of sin (cf. Rom. 5:12–21). If she did die, it was not because of her own sin but because she lived in a world still affected by sin. The Church has not determined whether or not Mary died before being assumed. The common view of theologians is that she did; however, the dogma of the Assumption assures us that she was taken up into heaven before her body could decay.

The evidence from history cited above begins in the sixth century. What did Christians believe before that time, from the first to the sixth centuries? We have fewer documents from this time, but they contain references to the Assumption. Even certain silences in these documents are suggestive. Normally, it is not wise to base one's conclusions on a lack of evidence, but sometimes the silence of the historical record speaks out with a loud voice. That is true of Mary's Assumption.

We have no evidence of Mary's relics (bones). This is extremely strange given two prominent practices of the early Christians. We know that Christians in the first few centuries would honor their dead by keeping their bones and personal possessions at a pilgrimage site, especially if the deceased was believed to have been a saint. We have evidence of these practices from every sector of ancient Christianity.

Yet strangely, at pilgrimage sites for Mary, both in Ephesus (where one tradition says she lived) and in Jerusalem (where another tradition places her), there are no bones. There also is no mention of them in the historical record, as there are for so many other great saints, including the apostles. This silence is doubly striking given the high esteem in which Mary was held by early Christians. Mary was considered the greatest saint. Yet no church, no town, and no individual has ever claimed to have her remains. None would have been regarded as more precious than hers, and surely we would have some historical references to her remains if their whereabouts had been known.

However, if Mary was assumed into heaven, body and soul, then of course there would be no record of her bones. This explains the periodic references made in the writings of Christians from these early centuries asserting that Mary had been taken into heaven uncorrupted.

In any case, it is clear that Pope Pius XII based his definition of the dogma on the faith of the Church from ancient times. However, the Pope also offered biblical reasons for the Assumption.

THE ASSUMPTION IN HOLY SCRIPTURE

There is no explicit statement of Mary's Assumption in the Bible for a good reason: The Bible is not a theological textbook. It is a record of God's dealings with his people up to a certain point, and it may well be that the last book of biblical history (Acts) was written before the Assumption even occurred. The Bible is an infallible revelation of God's being and love through the historical experiences of the people of God. There are many truths of the Christian faith that are not explicitly stated in Scripture. The Trinity is a good example. The Nicene Creed is another one—you will find no explicit confession of faith in Scripture, though every part is based on biblical revelation.

Mary's Assumption is another such case. Both the Old and New Testament Scriptures contain precedents for God assuming a person bodily into heaven. In Genesis 5:24 and Hebrews 11:5, we find that Enoch was taken to heaven without dying.

In 2 Kings 2:11, Elijah is assumed into heaven in a whirlwind. We read that, at the end of history, believers still living at that time will be caught up to meet the Lord in the air (cf. 1 Thess. 4:17). The idea of a bodily assumption is not foreign to the Bible at all.

Let us now look in more detail at one particular chapter of the New Testament: Revelation 12. Pick up your Bible and read with me. Revelation 12 tells the story of a woman who gives birth to a son who rules the nations with an iron rod. This woman is attacked by a dragon who attempts to kill her son and the other offspring that come from her. The story is set in fantastic imagery that is characteristic of apocalyptic literature. To understand it properly we must see the chapter in its place within the whole book.

The Revelation of John is structured on multiple sevens. In 5:1 we have the opening of the seven seals, the seventh of which is opened in 8:1. We discover that the opening of the seventh seal brings seven trumpets so that what we thought was the climax turns out to be a further development of God's plan. The seventh trumpet is sounded in 11:15. The seventh trumpet controls the interpretation of Revelation 12.

We are now looking at the climax of history for a second time in the book. We find out that this vision includes a peek into God's heavenly temple. We are now in the Holy of Holies. We read: "Then God's temple in heaven was opened, and the ark of his covenant was seen within his temple; and there were flashes of lightening, loud noises, peals of thunder, an earthquake, and heavy hail" (Rev. 11:19). This background sets the scene for the "sign of the woman."

If you now read Chapter 12 carefully, you will discover several things that point to Mary. Chapter 12:5 says that this woman gives birth to male child who "rules all with an iron rod." This is a quotation from Psalm 2:9. Long before Christ came, the Jews interpreted Psalm 2 as a Messianic psalm, and quoting from it shows that John wanted us to understand Jesus as the ruler with the iron rod.

This is confirmed when we read Revelation 19:15, where the same phrase refers unmistakably to Jesus. This means of course that the "woman clothed with the sun" refers in part to Mary (though it also may have other meanings as well, in keeping with Revelation's rich symbolism). This is the woman that is pursued by the dragon, also called the "ancient serpent" (Rev. 12:9), the Devil, and Satan. He is the accuser and deceiver.

This imagery places Mary squarely in the battle against evil, a warfare that began in Genesis 3:15:

I will put enmity between you and the woman,
and between your seed and her seed;
he shall bruise your head,
and you shall bruise his heel.

The offspring of the woman (i.e., Jesus Christ) destroys the work of the evil one (cf. 1 John 3:8). As Jesus is the New (second) Adam according to Paul (cf. Rom. 5:12–21), so Mary is the New Eve according to the Church Fathers. As the New Eve, she is united intimately with her Son for eternity.

This same woman has other offspring, too. They are named in Revelation 12:17 as "those who keep the commandments of God and bear testimony to Jesus." Similar phrases are used in Revelation 1:2 and 6:9 to refer to God's children. This means that Mary's children include the people of God, a truth that we have seen in earlier lessons. So, Revelation 12, while not telling us how Mary got to this heavenly position, clearly portrays her as the Mother of Jesus who is also our Mother, the Mother of believers. She is no ordinary mother.

> ## LUTHER ON THE QUEENSHIP OF MARY
>
> "She, the lady above heaven and earth, must have a heart so humble that she might have no shame in washing the swaddling clothes or preparing a bath for St. John the Baptist, like a servant girl. What humility! It would surely have been more just to have arranged for her a golden coach, pulled by 4,000 horses, and to cry and proclaim as the carriage proceeded, 'Here passes the woman who is raised above the whole human race!' She was not filled with pride by this immense praise: No woman is like unto thee! Thou art more than an empress or a queen blessed above all nobility, wisdom, or saintliness!" (Martin Luther, Sermon, Feast of the Visitation [1532], *Luther's Works* 21:327, 36:208, 45:107).

MARY, THE QUEEN OF HEAVEN?

In Revelation 12, we see the Mother of the Redeemer with a crown of twelve stars. A crown, of course, suggests two things: victory and royalty. We saw clearly how this chapter portrayed

Mary as a victor through the power of the male son she bore. But what about the other aspect of royalty? Do the Scriptures have anything to say about Mary's being Queen of Heaven?

Let us begin with the Old Testament because it always provides the background for understanding the New Covenant. It is especially here that we can expand our vision of the scriptural basis for the Marian dogmas.

During my journey to the Catholic Church, I was strongly impressed by the fact that our church backgrounds sometimes close us off to seeing the teachings of the Bible. I taught Protestant ministers the Old Testament for seven years in a seminary, but I never explored this aspect of Old Testament teaching. I was aware of the queen mother idea in ancient Israel, but I never once imagined that it had anything to do with Mary. When I encountered Catholic writers who connected the queen mother idea to Marian dogma and piety, I wondered to myself, "How could I have ever missed this?" Yet the answer was simple: My Christian experience to that point had been very limited. My church background simply never let me see it. In reality, the Catholic prayers invoking Mary as a queen were deeply rooted in the Bible.

Let us see how.

One of the clearest examples is David's wife and Solomon's mother, Bathsheba. We find Bathsheba sitting at her son's right hand:

> So Bathsheba went to King Solomon, to speak to him on behalf of Adonijah. And the king rose to meet her, and bowed down to her; then he sat on his throne, and had a seat brought for the king's mother; and she sat on his right. Then she said, "I have one small request to make of you; do not refuse me." And the king said to her, "Make your request, my mother; for I will not refuse you" (1 Kgs. 2:19–20).

Here is a clear picture of a queen mother who holds such influence with her son that, though he is king, he will not refuse her. The biblical writer uses the most amazing language when he says that King Solomon "bowed down" to his mother. This indicates profound reverence.

This position of queen mother went by a technical term in Hebrew. She was called the *gebirah*. This position was so important that when we are introduced to the kings of Judah in the book of Kings, it almost always mentions the name of the king's mother. This public institution was a type or foreshadowing of the New Covenant, in which the true king of Israel (Jesus) would come from the tribe of Judah to rule God's people.

This king would also have his mother sitting at his right hand. Now, we understand why the book of Revelation portrayed Mary as a queen with twelve stars. The number twelve is based on the twelve tribes of Israel and the twelve apostles of the new Israel. Mary, Jesus' own Mother, would be the *gebirah*, the Queen Mother of the New Covenant people of God.

Now we can appreciate why Catholics see in Mary such a sign of hope. Her Assumption is an ever-present reminder that Jesus is the ultimate victor. He is our king and conqueror; Mary is at his right hand just as he is at the right hand of the Father. Because Jesus is our hope and because she shares in his glory, she is a sign of our hope of sharing in Christ's heavenly glory.

STUDY QUESTIONS

Answers to multiple-choice, true/false, and factual-answer questions are found at the end of the book in Appendix 5.

1. In what way is Mary's Assumption related to Christ?

2. How does Mary's Assumption give us hope?

3. Mary was assumed into heaven:

   a) By her own power

   b) By the prayers of the saints

   c) By the power of Jesus' Resurrection

   d) All of the above

4. Must all Catholics believe in Mary's Assumption?

   YES _____ NO _____

5. By proclaiming Mary's Assumption, Pope Pius XII

   officially recognized something God had _____ done.

6. *Lex orandi, lex credendi* means:

   a) Let us pray

   b) Mary was assumed

   c) The prayer of the Church is the rule of faith

7. Why is the fact that there is no evidence of relics from

   Mary's life on earth support for Mary's Assumption?

   _____

   _____

   _____

   _____

MARY AMONG US

MARIAN APPARITIONS IN HISTORY

THROUGHOUT THIS BOOK we have been looking at what the Church teaches about Mary from the sources of public revelation (i.e., Scripture and Tradition). Public revelation is what God has revealed to the whole Church for all times and places until Christ comes again to end world history. Public revelation is binding on the Church and individual Catholics. The Church teaches that this public revelation ended with the death of the last apostle.

The dogma of the Assumption of Mary, which was formally defined in the twentieth century, does not conflict with this principle. That a dogma was articulated after the time of the apostles does not mean that it was not revealed to the apostles, but only that the Church had not proclaimed that particular doctrine in a definitive fashion. All the truths of the faith defined by the Church were revealed while Christ and his apostles were on earth, even if these truths did not receive a definitive proclamation until later.

The doctrine of the Trinity, for example, is implied in Scripture and Tradition but was not defined until the fourth century, when the Councils of Nicaea (A.D. 325) and Constantinople (A.D. 381) defined the divinity of Christ and the Holy Spirit on the basis of what was contained in public revelation.

Private revelations are of a completely different order. These are times when our Lord or one of his saints in heaven have appeared to people on earth—visually (apparitions), audibly (locutions), or both—to communicate a message that enables the faithful to live the Christian life more fully. Most frequently, these appearances have been of Mary.

These apparitions and locutions have usually been to a small group—to one person or to a few individuals. Sometimes these experiences are reported to Church authorities; the bishop of the diocese may investigate an appearance to determine its authenticity. At other times he refers the case to other authorities, such as the Holy See in Rome.

Private revelations are never judged to be necessary for the faith of the Church or even of an individual Catholic. The Church's approval does not mean that Catholics must believe them, but only that they are permitted to believe them because they do not conflict with any known dogma of the faith, and that there is evidence of their supernatural origin.

GETTING PERSPECTIVE ON PRIVATE REVELATIONS

The most important fact to understand is that the Church firmly believes that God guides the Church through the ages by the continuing ministry of the Holy Spirit (cf. John 14:26; 15:26–27; 16:13). This belief keeps the mind of the Church open to private revelations should God grant them through individuals. The Church does not want to quench the motions of the Spirit in the lives of its members (cf. 1 Thess. 5:19–21).

At the same time, the texts in the Gospel of John cited above make it clear that the Holy Spirit will not teach or reveal anything contrary to the teachings of Christ. As Jesus promised:

> I have yet many things to say to you, but you cannot bear them now. When the Spirit of truth comes, he will guide you into all the truth; for he will not speak on his own authority, but whatever he hears he will speak, and he will declare to you the things that are to come (John 16:12–13).

From this we can conclude that anything unveiled to individuals in a private form must conform to what we know is the teaching of Christ through the Church. The Second Vatican Council emphasizes this: "No new public revelation is to be expected before the glorious manifestation of our Lord Jesus Christ" (*Dei Verbum* 4).

Consequently, these private revelations do not belong to the "deposit of faith." Their sole purpose is to help people live in accord with the truths revealed in and by Christ:

Christian faith cannot accept "revelations" that claim to surpass or correct the revelation of which Christ is the fulfillment, as is the case in certain non-Christian religions and also in certain recent sects that base themselves on such "revelations" (CCC 67).

ST. JUAN DIEGO AND OUR LADY OF GUADALUPE

(1 5 3 1)

One of the most astounding Marian apparitions in the history of the Church took place in Mexico in 1531. According to the tradition, on December 9, 1531, a poor Aztec man named Juan Diego was walking near a hill at Tepeyac, just northwest of Mexico City. Suddenly, the Virgin Mary appeared to him.

Since Juan spoke no Spanish, the woman in the vision spoke to him in his native language, Nahuatl. She instructed him to tell the bishop that a chapel should be built on the site where Juan was standing. Juan obeyed the Lady's orders and went immediately to the bishop of Mexico City, whose name was Zumarraga.

Quite understandably, the bishop did not immediately believe Juan; he wanted some verification of the truth of Diego's claim that the Virgin had appeared to him.

On December 12, Diego returned to the same spot, and found roses blooming at a time of year when they normally would not. Mary appeared again to Juan and told him to pick some of the roses nearby as a sign to Bishop Zumarraga. Juan did so and went again to the bishop with the roses folded up in his outer garment, called a tilma.

When Juan opened up his tilma to pour out the roses on the bishop's desk, all those present saw the image of Our Lady of Guadalupe imprinted on Juan's tilma. One of those present was a young priest named Juan Gonzalez, who could speak both Spanish and Nahuatl and who acted as a translator. According to a summary written by Juan Gonzalez, both the bishop and Juan were amazed at the image they saw.

The historical basis of this account seems to be quite solid,

HOW DOES THE CHURCH DETERMINE THE AUTHENTICITY OF AN APPARITION OR LOCUTION?

The Church balances openness to the guidance of the Holy Spirit with a clear understanding of the finality and completeness of revelation in Christ. When the Church encounters one or more persons who claim to have seen Mary or one of the saints, the message is tested against the truths of public revelation. Then a judgment is made that falls into one of three categories.

1. When the Church believes that the private revelation is consistent with the deposit of faith, it renders a judgment known as Constat de Supernaturalitate (literally, "it agrees with the supernatural").

2. If there is certainty that the appearance cannot be attributed to supernatural phenomena, the Church renders the opposite judgment, Constat de Non Supernaturalitate ("it agrees with the non-supernatural"). In other words, there is a perfectly natural explanation of what happened in these apparitions.

3. When it cannot be established with certainty that the appearance was of supernatural origin, the Church renders a third type of judgment that falls between the first two: Non Constat de Supernaturalitate ("it does not agree with the supernatural").

This middle category of appearance is neither an approval nor a condemnation. An alleged apparition that has received this classification could still be approved or condemned at a later time if further action is taken.

Let us keep this understanding of how the Church judges private revelations in mind as we look at three of the most important Marian apparitions in history.

but perhaps the most astounding aspect of this event is the result. It is estimated that somewhere between nine and fifteen million Native American peoples converted to Christianity as a result of this apparition. After more than four centuries, the Shrine of Guadalupe is still the center of devotion among the Mexican people. No doubt part of this fervor is due to the preservation of Juan's tilma. After four centuries, Juan Diego's tilma is still intact, together with its image of the Virgin Mary, and remains on display in a basilica dedicated to Mary in Mexico City.

Scientists have been fascinated with the image of Our Lady

of Guadalupe. The colors and dyes on the tilma cannot be reproduced, and the image of Our Lady of Guadalupe is not a simple painting. Over twenty ophthalmologists have examined the eyes of Mary in the image, and have suggested that one can see the reflection of the people who were in the room when the image first appeared in 1531. This precise reflection, known as the "Samson Purkinje effect," is characteristic of all live human eyes. The amazing preservation of the tilma and the inexplicable way that the image was imprinted defy normal scientific explanation.

In 2002, Pope John Paul II canonized Juan Diego as a saint.

ST. BERNADETTE SOUBIROUS OF LOURDES AND THE IMMACULATE CONCEPTION

(1 8 5 8)

A second approved apparition of the Blessed Virgin Mary occurred in 1858. In Lesson 6, we studied how Pius IX defined the Immaculate Conception as a dogma of faith for all Catholics in 1854. However, given limited forms of communication in the nineteenth century, many Catholics in Europe had probably not heard about the definition, even four years later. This would have been especially true of uneducated people in remote rural villages (though the Immaculate Conception was already widely known and held as a doctrine).

Bernadette Soubirous was one such young lady. A poor farm girl of fourteen years, she could neither read nor write. On February 11, 1858, Bernadette was working near a stream where there was a grotto named Massabeille. Suddenly, she was transfixed by a vision of a lady bathed in light and wearing a white flowing garment. "This lady," as Bernadette called her, appeared to her eighteen times between February and July 11 of that same year. On March 25, the Feast of the Annunciation, the Lady dressed in white spoke to Bernadette in her local dialect of French, identifying herself by saying, "I am the Immaculate Conception." To the local bishop and many others, this seemed like a miraculous confirmation of the recently defined dogma.

During the time of Bernadette's visions and for many years thereafter, numerous miraculous cures were reported and verified. Today a large basilica stands at the sight of the apparitions and about two million pilgrims a year visit there. Many people have testified to the healing they have received from contact with the water that flows at Lourdes, and some of these miracles have been investigated and verified by Church authorities. More importantly, many more pilgrims have experienced profound spiritual conversion.

Bernadette was canonized as a saint in 1933 by Pope Pius XI.

THE CHILDREN OF FATIMA
AND
OUR LADY OF THE ROSARY

(1 9 1 7)

A third approved apparition took place at the end of the First World War, as the Bolshevik Revolution established the Soviet Union as a Communist state. Between May and October 1917, Mary appeared to three shepherd children in the parish of Fatima in the diocese of Leiria, Portugal. On the thirteenth day of each month, except August, Lucia Dos Santo, Francisco Marto, and Jacinta Marto reported the messages of a lady dressed in white who appeared to them identifying herself as Our Lady of the Rosary. The August apparition occurred on the nineteenth because the civil prefect of that area had kidnapped the children in order to interrogate them. In that apparition, Mary told the children that a great miracle would take place in October.

On October 13, about fifty thousand people gathered in the Cova da Iria, where the three children had first seen Mary. At noon that day, the sun appeared to shake, rotate violently, and then descend over the crowd before returning to normal. Many eye-witnesses gave accounts of this miracle and contributed to the establishment of this apparition when it was finally approved by the bishop of Leiria on October 13, 1930.

The message of the Fatima apparitions was remarkably relevant to those times. According to the children, Mary asked for cooperation in bringing peace to the world. This seemed to apply especially to Russia; at the time, Russia was involved in a revolution that would shape much of the twentieth century. When the Soviet Union finally collapsed in 1989, it seemed as if the promises of Fatima were coming true.

When Mary appeared at Fatima, she called for more prayer, penance, and sacrifice for the salvation of the world. The twentieth century has certainly been one of the bloodiest in history. But in the midst of these horrors, Fatima's message has instilled a spirit of prayer and sacrifice in the lives of millions.

In 2000, Pope John Paul II canonized two of the three children—Francisco and Jacinta—as saints. The third child, Lucia, is still alive and serving as a Carmelite sister in Portugal.

Appearances of Mary to people in the past and the present are evidences to strengthen our faith in God's promises. The Church never requires Catholics to believe in these apparitions, but it does allow us to embrace the practices of prayer and piety contained in them, as long as they are in accord with teachings of Christ expressed in Scripture as interpreted by the Church. Our faith can never be based on these private revelations, but it can be helped along the path toward greater devotion to God.

STUDY QUESTIONS

Answers to multiple-choice, true/false, and factual-answer questions are found at the end of the book in Appendix 5.

1. Public revelation is binding on the Church and the individual Catholic, but private revelations are never judged to be necessary for the faith of the Church or even an individual Catholic.

   TRUE _____   FALSE _____

2. It is possible for a private revelation to be truly of the Holy Spirit and teach or reveal something contrary to the

teachings of the Catholic Church.

TRUE _____ FALSE _____

3. Name three of the most important apparitions in history.

_____

_____

_____

4. Our Lady of Lourdes told Bernadette Soubirous, "I am the

_____ ."

5. Although our faith cannot be based on private revelation,

what can they help us to do?

_____

_____

_____

MARY IN OUR DAILY LIVES

THROUGHOUT THIS GUIDE we have been exploring the ways in which Mary affects our lives. We have discovered her importance for Catholics, and have attempted to understand the practical importance of Marian beliefs. At the same time, we need to consider how Mary is to play a part of our daily lives for one simple reason: The practices and beliefs we treasure most are those that somehow become a part of the fabric of our everyday lives. In this lesson, we want to find out how Mary can become an integral part of our daily devotional lives so that we can learn to live all that Jesus taught us (cf. Matt. 28:20).

Perhaps the most crucial truth to recall is that Mary always leads us to her Son Jesus Christ. Her motherhood was designed to give us Jesus Christ as our Savior. Her continuing motherly care for us individually and together as the Church is still meant to bring us closer to Christ.

SCARED OF DEVOTION TO MARY?

Some Christians, Catholics included, have doubts about devotion to Mary because they think that we should dedicate our lives to God alone. We can gain some clarity on Marian devotion by understanding some important distinctions in our prayer life.

It is absolutely true that the ultimate form of devotion should be reserved to God alone; no one can claim our affections completely except God. We can give total and complete love to Jesus Christ because he is God in the flesh. This kind of worship must be reserved for each member of the Holy Trinity.

Still, devotion to human beings is not strange to us at all. We admire a man who is devoted to his wife. We honor a woman who is devoted to the needs of her children. Even more, we honor our mothers for all that they have done for us. Our love for Mary should be like this, for she is our Mother in faith. The honor we give her is not worship, but it is a special attachment much like the attachment we have to our natural mothers.

The Church encourages us to look to Mary for help and ask for her intercession. We are able to do so because Mary continues to have a vital cooperative role in God's plan of salvation, just as when she gave God her "yes" to become the Mother of his Son. She also sustained fidelity to her Son throughout his thirty years of private life and the three years of his public ministry. Most of all, Mary stayed faithful to Jesus during his passion, death, and resurrection. After his Ascension into heaven, she remained faithfully with the Church.

Asking Mary's intercession is not an act of worshiping her. Much less is it the case that we Catholics worship statues, medals, scapulars, and rosaries. They have no magical power to save, but we have them near us—and often on us—as reminders of Mary's presence with us and how we are called to serve God and our neighbor in ways she exemplified so wondrously.

WALKING WITH MARY THROUGH THE YEAR

Loving Mary is not done only with words, but by living in her company. Perhaps the easiest way to do this is to follow the Church's yearly calendar and pay special attention to Marian feast days. This practice has the weight of history behind it. The Church's liturgical calendar has celebrated feast days dedicated to Mary since at least the fourth century.

In more recent times, Saturday has been set aside and honored as Mary's day, as it falls between Friday (the day of her Son's Crucifixion) and Sunday (the day of her Son's Resurrec-

**Hail Mary
(Ave Maria)**

Hail Mary, full of grace, the Lord is with thee. Blessed art thou amongst women, and blessed is the fruit of thy womb, Jesus. Holy Mary, Mother of God, pray for us sinners, now, and at the hour of our death. Amen.

tion). And every year the months of May and October are dedicated to her. The month of October is usually designated as the month of the rosary.

The Church has set aside a number of days to recall to our attention Mary and what God accomplished through her. Some of the most important Marian feast days are January 1 (Mary, the Mother of God), August 15 (the Assumption of Mary), and December 8 (the Immaculate Conception). These three are holy days of obligation in the United States, meaning Catholics are supposed to attend Mass on those days.

However, there are other important Marian days in the liturgical year as well. Some of them focus on events in Mary's life as recorded in the Bible (e.g., May 31, the Visitation; cf. Luke 1:39–56). Others celebrate Church-approved apparitions in Christian history (e.g., December 12, Our Lady of Guadalupe). For a full list of Marian feast days, see the appendix at the end of the lesson.

The Church's calendar helps us to develop a living relationship with Mary as the greatest of the saints. She can become a part of our thoughts as we worship God in the Mass. If you were to read a little about Mary on every feast day in honor of her during the year, your knowledge of her life and significance would grow. This in turn would foster a love for Mary as your Mother in faith.

THE ANGELUS

V: The angel spoke God's message to Mary,

R: and she conceived of the Holy Spirit. *Hail Mary . . .*

V: I am the lowly servant of the Lord:

R: Let it be done to me according to your word. *Hail Mary . . .*

V: And the Word became flesh

R: And lived among us. *Hail Mary . . .*

V: Pray for us, holy Mother of God,

R: That we may become worthy of the promises of Christ.

All: Lord, fill our hearts with your grace. Once, through the message of an angel you revealed to us the Incarnation of your Son; now, through his suffering and death lead us to the glory of his Resurrection. We ask this through Christ our Lord. Amen.

MARY'S PRESENCE IN OUR DAILY PRAYER LIFE

Mary's presence in our lives does not have to be limited to certain days of the year. Our fathers and mothers in faith—the great saints of the past—have given us numerous prayers involving Mary to illumine our minds and encourage our hearts. Not only does the use of these prayers unite us with Catholics in the past, it also unites us with Christians all over the world today. About 75 percent of the world's Christians are Catholic or Orthodox. Mary is an integral part of both these ancient traditions of Christianity, and both regularly invoke Mary's intercession.

One of these Marian prayers is known as the Angelus (see inset). This prayer, prayed in verse and response, has been said for centuries to commemorate the Incarnation of God in the womb of Mary. It is traditionally recited at 6:00 A.M., noon, and 6:00 P.M. If you study this prayer closely, you will see how deeply it is based on Scripture. Furthermore, you will notice how it emphasizes Mary's humility and how it focuses on the Incarnation, that act of the Son of God becoming man. This prayer clearly shows how prayers involving Mary are in fact really about her Son and to her Son.

Yet Catholic devotion is not limited to prayers involving Mary. The Church believes that it is proper to pray to God through Mary, much the same way we might ask other Christians on earth to pray for us. One famous prayer that invokes Mary's intercession is the Memorare. Composed in the twelfth century by the great French abbot St. Bernard of Clairvaux, it has become a classic, and is likely the most popular prayer other than the rosary in seeking Marian intercession.

> ## THE SCAPULAR
>
> The scapular was introduced in the early Middle Ages. It was a large and narrow cloth slipped over the head, and worn over the front and back of the religious habit, symbolizing the easy burden and yoke of Christ, while functionally keeping the habit clean. Gradually, the scapular decreased in size, and was commonly worn by the laity as a sign of devotion.
>
> Now, there exist no fewer than sixty-seven kinds of scapulars, each with different devotions and directions related to them. The most common of these is the brown scapular of Our Lady of Mount Carmel.

The most well-known Marian prayer is the rosary, a form of prayer that combines fundamental elements of Catholic worship with deep roots in Scripture and the Church. The prayer grew over the centuries from the simple beginnings of the sign of the cross in the first century and the Apostle's Creed (A.D. 125 in its earliest form). These practices continued as Christians prayed standard prayers such as the Lord's Prayer, which

THE ROSARY

The rosary is more than a set of individual prayers. It is a meditation on the central mysteries of Christianity. The rosary, said prayerfully, is a prelude to contemplative prayer. While Marian in structure, its purpose is to lead us into a deeper relationship with her Son, whose life is the principle subject of the mysteries on which the rosary focuses.

Until very recently, there were three sets of mysteries prayed in the rosary, each having five meditations.

The *joyful mysteries* have to do with the Incarnation and birth of Jesus:

The Annunciation (Luke 1:26–38)

The Visitation with Elizabeth (Luke 1:39–56)

The Birth of Jesus
(Luke 2:1–21; Matt.1:18–25)

The Presentation of Jesus in the Temple
(Luke 2:22–38)

The Finding of Jesus in the Temple
(Luke 2:41–51)

The *sorrowful mysteries* have to do with Jesus' passion and death:

Jesus' Sorrow in Gethsemane
(Luke 22:39–46)

The Scourging at the Pillar
(Matt. 27:26; John 19:1)

The Crown of Thorns (Matt. 27:29)

The Carrying of the Cross
(Luke 23:26–31; John 19:17)

The Crucifixion (Matt. 27:35–50;
Mark 15:24–37; Luke 23:33–46;
John 19:18–30)

The *glorious mysteries* have to do with Jesus' resurrection and glorification:

The Resurrection (Matt. 28:1–10; Mark 16:6;
Luke 24:5–7)

The Ascension into Heaven
(Acts 1:9–11; Mark 16:19)

The Descent of the Holy Spirit (Acts 2:1–4)

The Assumption of Mary
(cf. Rev. 12:1–17; Judith 15:9–10)

The Queenship of Mary (cf. Rev. 12:1–17)

In 2002, Pope John Paul II introduced the *luminous mysteries*, which have to do with the earthly ministry of Jesus.

The Baptism of Jesus (Matt. 3:13–17;
Mark 1:9–11; Luke 3:21–22)

The Wedding in Cana (John 2:1–11)

The Proclaiming of the Kingdom
(Matt. 10:7–8)

The Transfiguration (Matt. 17:1–9;
Mark 9:2–10; Luke 9:28–36)

The Institution of the Eucharist
(Matt. 26:26–29; Mark 14:22–25;
Luke 22:19–20)

The purpose of praying the rosary is to contemplate and thus come to participate in these mysteries. The Hail Marys are intended to ask Mary's intercession as we are led to a greater depth of meditation on salvation through Christ.

When the devotion of the rosary was introduced, when one prayed all three sets of the mysteries, one prayed 150 Hail Marys. This practice mirrored that of the monks, who pray the 150 psalms in the Divine Office. Since most ordinary people were illiterate in the Middle Ages, they could not read to pray the Divine Office and the psalms were too long for most people to memorize. So, the rosary became a way for common people to pray that reminded them of all that Christ had done for them.

is recorded in Scripture (cf. Matt. 6:9–13).

By about the fourth century, the Church added other small prayers such as the Minor Doxology in praise of the Trinity ("Glory Be"). To these were added a specifically Marian prayer known as the Hail Mary. The Hail Mary evolved into a single prayer from the sixth to the sixteenth century (see inset). The first half of the prayer was derived from the words of Scripture itself (cf. Luke 1:28, 42), while the second half reflected these biblical ideas of Christians praying for one another.

KEEPING MARY
CLOSE TO OUR HEARTS

One final way to grow in our love for Mary as Jesus' Mother is to keep pictures of her in our homes or carry them with us on our person. It is not strange at all to have reminders of someone we love close to us. It warms our hearts to look at these reminders and cherish our relationship with that person. One way to remind ourselves of Mary's presence is to wear a scapular (see inset).

In this lesson we have surveyed a number of ways that Mary can become a part of our daily lives through prayers that have been handed down throughout Church history. These prayers have the witness of history and the stamp of the Church's approval. The essence of this relationship with Mary is that of children to a mother. God the Father has given us a Mother to love us within the family of God. And not just any mother, but the Mother of Jesus. If we love Jesus, as every Christian should, we will love those who belong to Jesus. And who belongs to Jesus more intimately than Mary?

STUDY QUESTIONS

Answers to multiple-choice, true/false, and factual-answer questions are found at the end of the book in Appendix 5.

1. Mary always leads us to _____

_____ .

The Memorare

Remember, O most gracious Virgin Mary, that never was it known that anyone who fled to your protection, implored your help, or sought your intercession was left unaided. Inspired with confidence, I fly to you, O virgin of virgins, my Mother. To you I come, before you I stand, sinful and sorrowful. O Mother of the Word Incarnate, despise not my petitions, but in your mercy, hear and answer me. Amen.

2. Showing honor and devotion to another human being is not idolatry. In what ways do we show honor and devotion to others in the ordinary course of our lives?

_____

_____

_____

3. Name three Marian feast days and the doctrines that they celebrate, and explain how they relate to us.

_____

_____

_____

_____

_____

4. What percentage of the world's Christian population traditionally invokes Mary's intercession?

   a) 25%

   b) 50%

   c) 75%

5. According to the text, what is the purpose of praying the rosary?_____

_____

_____

APPENDIXES

APPENDIX 1: GLOSSARY

Almah Hebrew for "young woman" or "virgin." St. Matthew translated it in his Gospel as *parthenos*, which means only "virgin."

Angelus A traditional Catholic prayer said in the morning, at noon, and in the evening that focuses on the announcement of the birth of Christ to Mary. *Angelus* is the Latin word for "angel" and the first word of the prayer in that language. (See also Annunciation.)

Anne and Joachim Traditionally believed to be the parents of the Virgin Mary.

Annunciation The event recorded in Luke 1:26–38 in which the angel Gabriel announced to Mary that she would become the mother of the Redeemer. It is also the first mystery of the joyful mysteries of the rosary.

Apocalyptic An adjective derived from the Greek word for "revelation" or "unveiling." It describes a type of literature in the Bible that represents prophetic events symbolically. The book of Revelation is sometimes called "the Apocalypse."

Apparition A vision or other supernatural appearance of Christ, Mary, or one of the saints.

Ark of the Covenant The box used in the Old Testament tabernacle and Temple that was overlaid with gold. It contained the tablets of the Law, the manna, and the rod of Aaron that budded. It was seized in the Babylonian exile and lost forever.

Ascension Jesus' return to heaven forty days after his Resurrection (cf. Acts 1:1–11). This term is not used with regard to Mary.

Assumption The event in which the Blessed Virgin Mary was taken into heaven, body and soul, at the end of her earthly life.

Catacombs Underground caverns that were used by ancient Christians for burial. In times of persecution Christians worshiped in these caverns. It is estimated that there are over 150,000 Christians buried in the catacombs of Rome.

Chalcedon (Council of) The ecumenical council that met in A.D. 451 to define as infallible teaching the doctrine of Christ's two natures in one person.

Christotokos The term used by Nestorius to refer to Mary as the "Christ-bearer." Nestorius wrongly rejected the traditional title *Theotokos*, or "God-bearer."

Church Fathers The leaders of the Church from the first century until about A.D. 750. Their writings witness to the Church's beliefs, liturgies, and practices during this period.

Covenant A binding agreement between parties. In Scripture, covenants are regarded as sacred agreements. The term is often used to describe how God deals with Israel and the Church. It means a binding relationship between God and his people that is marked by mutual commitment, and accompanied by signs such as rituals and sacraments. In Scripture, the time of the Old Testament (Israel) is called the Mosaic Covenant, and the time of the New Testament (Church) the New Covenant.

Daughter of Zion An expression in the prophets of the Old Testament referring to Israel. This imagery plays into the Catholic understanding of Mary as the archetypal daughter of Israel, the obedient servant who comes to do God's will.

Divine Office The prescribed prayers of priests and religious throughout the Church to be said at appointed times during the day (e.g., morning and evening prayers). Also called the Liturgy of the Hours.

Dogma A doctrine that has been infallibly taught to be "of the faith" (Latin, *de fide*). This is the highest level of doctrine held by the Church. All Catholics are bound to believe the dogmas of the Church. It derives from the Greek word meaning "belief" or "teaching."

Dormition of Mary The Sleep of Mary. Celebrated as a feast in the Eastern parts of the Church on August 15.

Dulia A kind of devotion or honor that is appropriate to one of the saints. (See also *hyperdulia*.)

Ecumenical council A worldwide council of bishops, together with the pope, whose authority is binding on the entire Church. The first one was at Nicaea in A.D. 325. The most recent ecumenical council was Vatican II in the 1960s.

Encyclical A circular letter (letter to be circulated) written and issued by the pope and usually addressed to the bishops of the world. In encyclicals some aspect of Church teaching is presented.

Fiat The Latin word that means "let it be." It is used in Genesis 1 when God says, "Let there be light," etc. It is also used by Mary in Luke 1:38 when she says to Gabriel, "Let it be to me according to your word."

Firstborn The term used of Jesus Christ in the Bible (e.g., Luke 2:7). The firstborn son of a mother held a special place in ancient Israelite families that carried with it particular rights and duties. His birth was an occasion of special celebration. As a result, a child would be designated as the firstborn even if there were no subsequent children from the union.

Gebirah A Hebrew word used in the Old Testament meaning "Great Lady" and used more specifically to refer to the queen mother (cf. 1 Kings 2:19–20). The queen mother held the most authoritative position in the royal family after the king. This provides the biblical foundation for understanding Mary as the Queen Mother of the Redeemer who rules with her Son from heaven.

Holy day of obligation A day in which Catholics are required to attend Mass. Every Sunday is a day of obligation. There are other holy days for the universal Church and others that are for specific countries.

Hyperdulia The kind of devotion appropriate to the Blessed Virgin Mary. It is distinguished from *dulia*, which is devotion to the saints, and from *latria* (worship appropriate to the triune God alone). As the name suggests, *hyperdulia* is a form of *dulia* that is above the ordinary level of *dulia*. It is shown to Mary because she is the greatest of the saints, having been the vessel through which God became incarnate as man.

Idolatry The act or practice of worshiping an idol (i.e., a statue that is regarded as a god), which is forbidden in the first commandment. If one were to worship statues of the saints or Mary (or even statues of Jesus or the Father) as if they were gods, then one would be committing idolatry. However, Catholics have a clear understanding that statues are symbols and not divinities.

Immaculate Conception The act of God's grace whereby he protected the Virgin Mary from contracting original sin and its stain (Latin, *macula*) at the moment of conception in her mother's womb.

Incarnation The historically unique event of the second Person of the Trinity, the Logos, becoming man. It is a foundational event of salvation history.

Infallible The quality of being unable to err. Christ willed that his Church have the attribute of infallibility in defining matters of faith and morals, thereby protecting and preserving the

Church in the truth. One way in which the Church's infallibility can be exercised is through the *ex cathedra* definitions of the pope as universal pastor and teacher.

Intercession Praying or asking on behalf of another person. In particular, interceding with God on behalf of his people or a person. Mary, the saints, and angels are intercessors in heaven because they pray for people on earth.

Kecharitomene The Greek word in Luke 1:28 that is usually translated "full of grace." It is used as a way of addressing Mary by the angel Gabriel and indicates her unique state of having been graced by God.

Latria Worship that is due to God alone. It contrasts with *dulia* (devotion to the saints), and *hyperdulia* (devotion to the Blessed Virgin Mary, the greatest of all the saints).

Lex orandi, lex credendi The principle of Catholic theology that roughly means, "The law of prayer is the law of faith." It points to the fact that doctrines of the faith are to be found in the historical liturgies of the Church. The Church's Marian dogmas have manifold witnesses in the liturgy of the Church.

Litany A responsive prayer of petitions (such as the Litany of the Blessed Virgin Mary) to God, saints, and angels.

Liturgy The official public worship offered to God by the Church in the sacraments and the liturgy of the hours. It derives from a Greek word meaning "public service" and was the most common word used in ancient Christianity for public worship.

Locution A supposed act of God or one of the saints speaking to a person on earth.

Lourdes The place in France where St. Bernadette saw the vision of the Blessed Virgin Mary in 1858.

Magnificat Mary's song recorded in Luke 1:46–55. The title is based on her words "My soul magnifies [Latin, *magnificat*] the Lord, and

my spirit rejoices in God my savior." This prayer displays insightful understanding of redemptive history, her faith in trusting the goodness of God. It also shows her humility in that, even carrying the Messiah himself, she calls herself the lowly handmaid of God.

Marialis Cultus "Devotion to Mary."

Messiah An English transliteration of the Hebrew word *Meshiach*, meaning "Anointed One." The Greek word *christos* ("Christ") means the same thing. Jesus the Christ is the long awaited Savior of Israel.

Mother of God The title used among the Church Fathers to emphasize her carrying God the Son within her womb. This was defined infallibly at the Council of Ephesus in A.D. 431. Also called divine maternity.

Munificentissimus Deus "The most generous God." In this 1950 document, Pope Pius XII solemnly defined *ex cathedra* the doctrine of the Assumption of Mary, body and soul, into heaven.

Mystery A truth that cannot be known by human reason alone and must be revealed to man by God. Alternately, a truth rich in spiritual meaning that cannot be fully grasped by the human intellect. It also refers to the fifteen major points of meditation in the rosary.

Nicaea (Council of) Traditionally called the first ecumenical council, which defined the doctrine of the Trinity in A.D. 325.

Order of Grace God's way of dealing with us in the Christian life. Just as there is a natural order consisting of physical laws, so there is a supernatural order consisting of God's dealings with us in grace. In the order of grace, Mary is the Mother of all Christians.

Original sin The deprivation of the grace that God gave to our first parents in paradise. Associated with it is the stain of original sin, which is a corruption of human nature. Both original sin and its stain are passed on to all humans as a result of the fall of man. Baptism removes original sin by supplying the soul with sanctifying grace. It does not remove the stain of original sin. By the Immaculate Conception, God protected Mary from both original sin and its stain.

Orthodox Adhering to right beliefs. It contrasts with heterodoxy or heresy.

Paschal Mystery The redemptive work of Jesus from the Last Supper through and including the Resurrection. The term is used to refer to the mystery in which Christ himself served as God's Paschal (Passover) Lamb to save us from our sins.

Perpetual virginity The doctrine that Mary remained a virgin throughout her life, and thus had no children other than Jesus.

Piety The way in which a person lives out his spirituality. The word derives from a Latin word meaning "devotion." Marian piety consists of devotion to the Mother of God.

Pilgrimage A journey to a holy site for prayer and spiritual growth.

Redemptoris Mater Literally means "Mother of the redeemer," referring to Mary. It is the title of one of John Paul II's encyclicals.

Relic A possession or body part of a saint.

Revelation (private) Truths revealed to and intended for a particular person to assist him in living the Christian life. No one is required to believe them except the recipient. They cannot correct or extend the dogmas of the faith.

Revelation (public) Eternal truths revealed by Christ and taught by his apostles, the deposit of faith. These teachings are in Scripture and the Apostolic Tradition passed down through the centuries in the Church. All Catholics are required to accept what has been revealed in public revelation.

Rosary A form of prayer used since the Middle Ages that employs beads for praying. There are three cycles of the rosary: the joyful mysteries, the sorrowful mysteries, and the glorious mysteries. Each cycle consists of praying the Our Father, the Hail Mary, and the Glory Be. Often the rosary is concluded by saying the Hail Holy Queen.

Sacrament An outward, physical sign instituted by Christ as a vessel of inward, spiritual grace. There are seven sacraments: baptism, confirmation, Eucharist, reconciliation (penance, confession), the anointing of the sick, holy orders (ordination), and holy matrimony.

Saint A person or angel whom the Church has declared to be in heaven.

Sanctified The state of being holy. Alternately, dedicating a person or object to holiness.

Sanctifying Grace The grace that God gives to the soul that enables it to have union with God and salvation.

Theotokos The traditional term used of Mary reaffirmed by the Council of Ephesus in A.D. 431 meaning "God-bearer." *Theotokos* emphasizes that Mary had God in her womb.

Tilma The cloak worn by St. Juan Diego on which was imprinted the image of Our Lady of Guadalupe in 1531 and now hangs in the basilica in Mexico City.

Tradition From a Latin word meaning "handing on." Catholic theology derives its teachings from both Scripture and Tradition. It also distinguishes Tradition (an infallible teaching that must be believed) from tradition (a practice that may be practiced). Those teachings handed on from the apostles are regarded as Apostolic or Sacred Tradition and must be adhered to.

Appendix 2: Citations

SCRIPTURE
Old Testament
Genesis
3:15
5:24
12:5
13:8

Exodus
20:3, 4
25:10–22
25:22
40:34–38

Numbers
17:1–11

Deuteronomy
5:7, 8

2 Samuel
6
6:2

1 Kings
2:19–20
8:10, 13

2 Kings
2:11

Psalms
2:9

Wisdom
1:4

Isaiah
6:1–3
7:14

New Testament
Matthew
1:18
1:20
1:22, 23
1:25

5:8
5:48
6:9–13
12:46–50
13:55–56
27:26, 29
28:1–10, 20

Mark
3:31–34
10:45

Luke
1:26
1:26–38
1:28
1:28, 38
1:29
1:30
1:31, 32
1:34
1:35
1:38
1:39–45
1:39–56
1:41, 42
1:42
1:42, 48
1:42, 43
1:46, 47
1:48
1:50–55
2:1–21
2:19, 51
2:22–38
2:34, 35
2:35
2:41–52
22:39–46
23:26–31
23:32–42

John
1:11
1:11, 12
1:12
1:14

2:1–12
2:25
2:3
2:3–5
2:4
2:5
3:1–3
14:6
14:17
14:26
15:26
15:26, 27
16:12
16:13
17:20
19:25–27
19:26
19:27

Acts
1:6–11
1:14
2:1–4
6:8

Romans
3:23
5:12
5:12–21
8:17
8:29
8:35–39

1 Corinthians
13:13
15:20, 23
15:21–22, 45

2 Corinthians
3:18

Galatians
4:4

Ephesians
1:6

4:1–6
19

1 Thessalonians
4:17

2 Timothy
4:6–8

Hebrews
2:12
11
11:5

1 John
3:8
4:11

Revelation
1:2, 9
5:1
6:9
8:1
9
11:15
11:19
12
12:1–17
12:1
12:5
12:17
19:15

*CATECHISM OF
THE CATHOLIC
CHURCH*
47
48
66
67
498
964
969

APPENDIX 3: MARIAN FEAST DAYS

The following are the feasts currently celebrated in the United States:

January 1 Mary, Mother of God (holy day of obligation)

February 2 The Presentation of the Lord (and Purification of the Blessed Virgin)

February 11 Our Lady of Lourdes (optional memorial)

March 25 The Annunciation

May 31 The Visitation

Saturday after the Feast of the Sacred Heart of Jesus Immaculate Heart of Mary

July 16 Our Lady of Mount Carmel (optional memorial)

August 5 Our Lady of the Snows (dedication of St. Mary Major Church, optional memorial)

August 15 The Assumption of Mary (holy day of obligation)

August 22 The Queenship of Mary (memorial)

September 8 The Birth of Mary

September 15 Our Lady of Sorrows (memorial)

October 7 Our Lady of the Rosary (memorial)

November 21 The Presentation of Mary (memorial)

December 8 The Immaculate Conception (holy day of obligation)

December 12 Our Lady of Guadalupe (memorial)

Saturday within the octave of Christmas (or if there is no Sunday within the octave)

December 30 Feast of the Holy Family

Saturdays may be observed as commemorations of the Blessed Virgin Mary when no other obligatory commemoration is scheduled.

APPENDIX 4: WHERE TO LEARN MORE

Key Works and Recommended Reading

Reginald Garrigou-Lagrange,
The Mother of the Savior
(Rockford, IL: TAN, 1994)

Scott Hahn, *Hail, Holy Queen*
(New York: Doubleday, 2001)

Kenneth J. Howell, *Mary of Nazareth*
(Santa Barbara, CA: Queenship Publishing Company, 1998)

Alfred McBride, *Images of Mary*
(Cincinnati, OH: St. Anthony Messenger Press, 1999)

Heidi Hess Saxton, *With Mary in Prayer*
(Chicago: Loyola Press, 2002)

APPENDIX 5:
ANSWERS TO STUDY QUESTIONS

LESSON 1: Our Mother in Faith

1. d)
2. The most common misunderstanding is that Catholics worship Mary. The best way to counteract this misunderstanding is to learn what the Church teaches about Mary, and to help others do the same. Learn to explain the difference between honoring Mary (as we honor other beloved people in our lives) and worship, which belongs only to God and never to a created being.
3. *Latria* is worship, which belongs to God alone. *Dulia* is the kind of honor or devotion given to the saints or to others we love, particularly those who have gone ahead of us to heaven. *Hyperdulia* is the special kind of honor we offer to Mary as our Mother in heaven and the greatest of the saints.
4. Mary, who needed a Savior just as all humans do.
5. Give ourselves completely to God's service, like Mary in Luke 1:38; contemplate the mysteries of salvation, like Mary in Luke 2:19, 51; obey God in everything, like Mary tells us in John 2:5; be faithful, even during hardship, as Mary did at the foot of the cross in John 19:25–27.
6. d)

LESSON 2: Mary in God's Plan of Salvation

1. True.
2. Israel.
3. Mary would break the curse of sin that originated with Eve. In other words, Mary is the New Eve.
4. False.
5. Mary. Jesus turned water into wine.
6. Because we see that Jesus honored his Mother's intercession by performing the first miracle of his public life. This should give us courage to ask for her intercession, trusting that Jesus will continue to honor his Mother's requests on our behalf.

LESSON 3: The Mother of God

1. "The mother of my Lord" acknowledged the divine presence in Mary's womb.
2. Here are some comparisons. More are possible: The ark was made of pure materials; Mary was also a pure vessel. The ark carried the Ten Words of God (Decalogue); Mary carried *the* Word of God. The ark was a symbol of God's word and presence; through Mary, God became present in her and in the world. The ark contained the Old Covenant; Mary contained the New Covenant.
3. The word *episkiasei* comes from a root word meaning "a shadow" or "a cloud" and is used to describe a visible cloud that descended over the tabernacle and the Temple in the Old Testament. Both were places of God's special presence. Luke wanted us to understand that God was in Mary's womb.
4. b)
5. *Christotokos*: Christ-bearer (bearer of only the human nature of Jesus).
Theotokos: God-bearer (bearer of both the human and divine natures). The first term recognizes only that Mary bore a man from her womb, while the second acknowledges that Mary bore God from her womb. To deny that Mary bore God from her womb would leave us with a savior who was not really God. As Pope Leo the Great said, "If Mary did not unite the Second Person of the Trinity to our humanity in her womb, then there really was no such person as the God-Man. And if there is no God-Man, then there can be no union between God and man. The only way for us to be united to God is for God to unite himself to us."
6. The mingling of water with the wine during the Mass represents us being able to share in the divinity of Christ, who humbled himself to share in our humanity.

LESSON 4: The Mother of the Church

1. True.
2. "Behold your mother. . . . Behold your son."
3. b)

4. John.

5. The human nature he took from Mary.

6. Romans 8:35–39: "Who shall separate us from the love of Christ? Shall tribulation, or distress, or persecution, or famine, or nakedness, or peril, or sword? As it is written, 'For thy sake we are being killed all the day long; we are regarded as sheep to be slaughtered.' No, in all these things we are more than conquerors through him who loved us. For I am sure that neither death, nor life, nor angels, nor principalities, nor things present, nor things to come, nor powers, nor height, nor depth, nor anything else in all creation, will be able to separate us from the love of God in Christ Jesus our Lord."

LESSON 5: Mary, Ever Virgin

1. True.

2. c)

3. Prayers in Eastern rite liturgy from the fourth century allude to Mary's perpetual virginity, as do various Eastern fathers.

4. Luther, Calvin.

5. d)

6. Many possible answers, including: The cross, a sign of defeat, brought victory over sin and evil; the last shall be first; the humble shall be exalted; the meek shall inherit the earth; the Creator became part of his creation; the King of the universe allowed himself to be subject to humans.

LESSON 6: The Immaculate Conception

1. c)

2. False.

3. a)

4. "Full of grace."

5. Mary's being preserved from original sin was accomplished in anticipation of her Son's redemptive work on the cross. In other words, Jesus is also Mary's Savior. Because of what he would do, this grace could be given to her in advance. Time limits us, but not God.

6. We see that Christ's perfect life, death and resurrection are the source of Mary's purity of heart, and if we are to become pure, it is only through the same source: Christ himself.

LESSON 7: The Assumption and Queenship

1. It is related to Jesus' Resurrection and Ascension.

2. Mary received in advance an aspect of salvation that is promised to all believers. It is the fulfillment of what is promised to us.

3. c)

4. Yes.

5. Already.

6. c)

7. Early Christians considered Mary the greatest saint. Yet, no church, no town, and no individual has ever claimed to have her remains. If Mary was assumed into heaven body and soul, no remains would be left on earth.

LESSON 8: Mary among Us: Marian Apparitions in History

1. True.

2. False.

3. Our Lady of Guadalupe, Fatima, Lourdes.

4. Immaculate Conception.

5. Have a greater devotion to God.

LESSON 9: Mary in Our Daily Lives

1. Christ.

2. Some answers are: devotion to a spouse; a woman's devotion to the needs of her children; honoring our mothers and fathers for all that they have done for us; honoring heroes who displayed self-sacrifice for the good of others.

3. Some answers are:

The Solemnity of Mary, the Mother of God (January 1): celebrates the Incarnation and Mary as *Theotokos* (God-bearer), assuring us that our redemption was accomplished by Jesus who was fully God and fully man.

The Assumption of Mary (August 15): celebrates Mary's body and soul being assumed into heaven at the end of her earthly life. This gives us hope that someday our souls will be reunited with our glorified bodies in heaven.

The Immaculate Conception (December 8): celebrates Mary's freedom from original sin from the moment of her conception, because the fruits of her Son's redemption were applied to her in anticipation of her special role as Mother of God. Her purity, because of Christ's redemption, is a hope of our redemption and the purity we can obtain through Jesus.

4. c)

5. To meditate on the central mysteries of Christianity, and lead us into a deeper relationship with Christ.

About the Author

KENNETH J. HOWELL is director of the John Henry Cardinal Newman Institute of Catholic Thought and adjunct associate professor of religious studies at the University of Illinois at Champaign-Urbana, where he teaches classes on the history, theology, and philosophy of Catholicism. He is the author of *Mary of Nazareth: Sign and Instrument of Christian Unity* and *God's Two Books: Copernican Cosmology and Biblical Interpretation in Early Modern Science*. Before entering the Catholic Church in 1996, he was a Presbyterian minister for eighteen years and a theological professor in a Protestant seminary.

ARE YOU READY TO LEARN MORE?

Congratulations for having completed the *Meeting Mary: Our Mother in Faith* learning guide in the Catholic Century Learning Series. Your diligent study will now help you answer your own and others' questions about this aspect of the Catholic faith with greater confidence.

Now that you have finished one study, make sure you look into *The Papacy*, our learning guide on the Chair of Peter. When you have finished this guide, you will be able to respond intelligently to questions about this important institution.

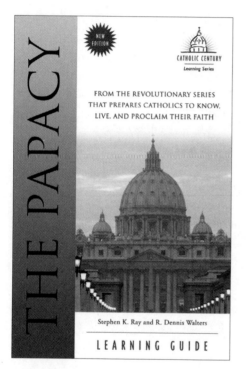

You'll discover the scriptural basis for:

✝ **The institution of the papacy**

✝ **Papal authority**

✝ **Papal infallibility**

✝ **Papal succession**

Have friends with questions on the papacy? Want to share your newfound knowledge with non-Christians, other Christians, and even interested Catholics? Consider purchasing multiple copies of *The Papacy* evangelization guide, a small booklet written to reach those with little or no knowledge of this key element of the Catholic Church.

For FREE information about this and other titles in our Catholic Century Learning Series, contact us:

Phone: (toll free) **1-888-291-8000**—U.S. only; 1-619-387-7200—International sales
Fax: 1-619-387-0042
Web: shop.catholic.com
Order Form: See the following page

Order now and we'll immediately send you the material you need to learn and share your faith with others.

ORDER FORM

ITEM #	TITLE	QTY	PRICE	TOTAL
CB001	**The Papacy learning guide** Improve your command of the biblical basis for the institution of the papacy, infallibility, papal authority, etc. Affordable, easy to use.		$7.95	
CB273	**The Papacy evangelization guide** At 32 pages, a perfect way to help others learn about this essential Catholic truth.		$1.95	
CB278	**Meeting Mary learning guide** Learn the truth behind the Church's teachings on Mary, from the early Church Fathers up through modern apparitions.		$7.95	
CB279	**Meeting Mary evangelization guide** Perfect for non-Catholics who want an easy way to learn about Mary for themselves.		$1.95	
CB021	**Pillar of Fire, Pillar of Truth** At 32 pages, Pillar is packed with information about the Catholic Church and God's plan for us. Powerful, yet concise!		$1.95	
CB208	**12 Painless Ways to Evangelize** Think it's tough? Here are a dozen quick and painless ways to get the Word out daily!		$1.95	
CT400	**Mega-Tract Pak** Explore 120 hot topics essential to Catholics in the modern world.		$29.95	

Ordering is Fast, Safe, Easy!

CALL: **1-888-291-8000** (M–F, 9 A.M.–5 P.M., Pacific Time)

WEB: **http://shop.catholic.com**

TAX: Calif. only: 7.75%	
S&H: $4.95 + 10%	
TOTAL:	

SHIP TO:

Name:

Address:

City:

State/Province: Zip/Postal Code: Country:

PAYMENT:

Check #:   Amount: Bank:

Credit Card: ☐ VISA   ☐ MasterCard   ☐ Discover

Number: -   -   -   Expires: /

Signature:

Catholic Answers ✛ 2020 Gillespie Way ✛ El Cajon, CA 92020
Main: 619-387-7200 ✛ Fax: 619-387-0042 ✛ Sales: 1-888-291-8000

CATHOLIC ANSWERS

Who We Are

Catholic Answers is the largest Catholic apologetics and evangelization organization in North America. We are lay people devoting our full-time efforts to promoting the Catholic faith through books, tracts, tapes, radio, magazines, and parish seminars.

Our Beliefs and Goals

We believe the Catholic Church was established by Jesus Christ and teaches the fullness of Christian truth. We want to spread the Catholic faith—by helping good Catholics become better Catholics, by bringing former Catholics "home," and by resolving misconceptions non-Catholics may have about the Church and what it teaches.

CATHOLIC ANSWERS, INC.
P. O. Box 199000, San Diego, California 92159-9000
(888) 291-8000 (U.S. orders)
(619) 387-7200 (int'l. orders)
(619) 387-0042 (fax)
www.catholic.com (web)